PALESTINE

IN NEED OF A JUST GOD

TERRELL E. ARNOLD

Copyright © 2011 Terrell E Arnold
All rights reserved.

ISBN: 1-4662-8181-2
ISBN-13: 9781466281813

Table of Contents

	Acknowledgments	vii
	Preface	ix
1.	Palestine—The Place and the People	1
2.	Clueless in Gaza	25
3.	Time to Grow up	31
4.	Collective Punishment Is Wrong	39
5.	The Recognition Stumbling Block	49
6.	Forcibly Renew the Insurgency	57
7.	The Diplomacy of Sticks and Stones	65
8.	"It Really Is That Simple"	79
9.	HR 4681—For Terrorism—Against the Palestinian People	93
10.	Palestinian Repression—The Intended Consequences	99
11.	Lebanon—The Israeli Game Plan	109
12.	Bush & Blair—Lebanon Is Not a Video Game	119
13.	The IDF Should Do the Numbers	125
14.	US-French Ceasefire Agreement Not Good Enough	129
15.	The Israeli/American Terrorism Generator	135
16.	The Partners to War Crime in the Holy Land	143
17.	Palestine—Peace Not Apartheid	155

18.	Zionism and the Birth of Middle East Terrorism	159
19.	Palestine—An Honorable Solution	173
20.	The Ethnic Cleansing of Palestine	187
21.	Palestine—In Need of a Just God	191
22.	Gaza's Tragic Link to the West's Terrorism Mindset	205
23.	Hamas—A Political Portrait	219
24.	The Hobson's Choice of Hamas	225
25.	Linking Palestine to Iran	233
26.	Jerusalem—Historical Disaster in the Making	241
27.	Palestine and the Demise of Conscience	253
28	Zionists Fabricate as US Digs a Deeper ME Hole	261
29.	The Road to Middle East Peace	269

Annexes		283
I.	Balfour Declaration	285
II.	Bush letter to Sharon	287
III.	Sharon letter to Bush	291
IV.	Gist of House-Senate Resolution	295
V.	UNSC Resolution 242	297
VI.	UNSC Resolution 338	301
VII.	Ron Paul Statement to House	303
VIII.	Biographic sketches	305

Acknowledgments

A book of this type cannot be written without inputs from a wide range of sources. Many of those sources are hidden in the ways other writers refer on the Internet to the roots of their materials. Some contributors simply do not wish to be mentioned by name, and that is particularly true of controversial subjects such as Palestine. With that in mind, six people are worthy of special mention: Amy Rabas, graduate of the University of Wisconsin Stevens Point, and now a practicing Chicago designer, earned my admiration and gratitude for the book cover she created out of the very chaos of the Palestinian environment. Jeff Rense, who has worked the issues often in radio broadcasts with me, and whose website *rense.com* has published all the dated articles in this collection, makes a tremendous daily contribution to a worldwide informed public. Alex Noble, a longtime friend and adviser on marketing, provided practical advice on how to approach the market for works of this character to assure the word gets to its audience. Former Ambassador Holsey Gates Handyside, an experienced Middle East hand, contributed much to accuracy and perspective. Robert Stiver, a passionate activist for the people and land of Palestine and an avid exploiter of the cable-adjunct public-access TV medium, provided much insightful editorial support, while contributing always to the morale of the writer. And finally, my wife Yvonne, who has endured my preparations for lectures, speeches and writings for much of our long and happy marriage, can take pride in the editorial feel she has given this work. There are many others, and I will thank them as I see them.

Preface

Palestine is a difficult country to write about. That is not because the problem is complicated. It is not. For almost a century the inhabitants of Palestine have been losing control of their homeland. That is the long and the short of it. The hard part is dealing with that reality: The systematic theft of Palestinian land, the ethnic cleansing of the Palestinian people, the harsh business of introducing a new race, the Ashkenazim (Khazar) Jews, into Palestine, and their excruciating processes of Palestinian dispossession. In their effort to claim Palestine, the Ashkenazim have raised the discredited practice of 19th Century colonialism and its inherent racism to new and disturbing levels in the "Holy" Land.

The principal burden posed for any writer on this subject is that any discussion of the Palestine situation must be "balanced". The presentational key to this journalistic challenge is that if you say anything possibly unpleasant or nasty about the Israelis, you must be equally nasty to the Palestinians. In this lexicon, balance in reporting or commentary finds itself, inevitably, in conflict with truth—because, simply put, there can be no balance in an equation where the strong pretend they have no equals. If the imperative is to avoid any embarrassing confrontation with reality, in this peculiar realm much that is important gets left unsaid because it might be "offensive". It is by these peculiar verbal antics that the efforts to make peace in the Middle East become a process, not an outcome.

This book looks at the situation frankly from a Palestinian perspective. While Jews and Judaism are not topics for discussion, Zionist nationalism and the efforts of the Ashkenazim European Jews to take Palestine away from its people must be squarely faced. In light of that Ashkenazim campaign, after six decades of unremitting pressure, Palestine has become the vortex of an unstable and increasingly desperate human tragedy. As surrounding countries and their governments comprehend all too well, events in Palestine tend to boil over across borders, to become factors in political and social developments in the larger neighborhood. Sometimes those reverberations work to the advantage of the people of Palestine. Sometimes they work for the Israelis.

The goal of this book is to stick to the facts, many of which unfortunately are unpleasant. The picture fits a reality that is biased by the fact that a strong European origin group (the Ashkenazim) is engaged in taking Palestine from the indigenous peoples who have lived there for millennia. The outsiders involved (the United States and the Ashkenazim mainly) make this situation potentially explosive by insisting that the Palestinian people have no right to resist.

Until recently, groups in surrounding countries that strongly support or sympathize with the Palestinian people have made their governments nervous. That concern was not about any possibility that the Palestinians might attack; it rather centered on prospects that militants such as the Muslim Brotherhood in Egypt—which is credited with inspiring formation of the Palestinian group Hamas—may develop sufficient political strength to challenge present oligarchic governments. Both Tunisia and Egypt appear to be in early if ill-defined stages of that transition. Several other countries are struggling with transition, but the seriousness and timing of change are unclear. A rebellion that started on the ground in Libya has now been fed by imports and turned into a US/NATO and Arab activist invader led war against Moammer Qaddafi. What might have been a natural part of an Arab Spring has become an outsider interference. Both the nature and control of future Libyan leadership are now in formative stages, but the roles of outsiders are presently dominant. Whether or how the Palestinians might benefit from the Arab Spring remains uncertain.

Much of this book focuses on issues and developments during the past six years leading up to and following (a) the Palestinian election of January 2006, (b) Israel's 2006 invasions of Lebanon and Gaza, (c) the early and continuing US/Israeli effort to ignore and overturn the Hamas election victory (d) the lead up to and execution of Israel's 2008-09 assault on Gaza and the ongoing strangulation of its landmass and people, (e) the beginning of Obama administration efforts to cope with the problems of Middle East peace, (f) the current efforts of Israeli Prime Minister Netanyahu to expel the Palestinians from East Jerusalem and erase the historic signs of their presence, and (g) the growing signs of instability and unraveling in Israel itself. All of those developments affect the prospects of any viable future for the Palestinian people and any likelihood of an enduring peace in their homeland.

Chapter 1.
Palestine—The Place and the People

What is Palestine? This small piece of land figures in our lives in many ways, and it is easy to assume we know the place, even if we don't know exactly where it is. Specifically named or not, it is the center of the Middle East Arab/Israeli conflict. Several of the world's most ancient cities such as Tyre, Byblos, Gaza, Jerusalem and Bethlehem are in the region. Referred to by many as the Holy Land, it is the most important single place in the Christian tradition. It also contains one of the three most sacred sites in Islam, the al Aqsa Mosque. And of course it includes the site of ancient Israel and it is central to the Jewish experience. The site figures in Biblical prophecy as surrounding the Temple Mount, the focus of Daniel's prophecies of the End of Days. Historically it was at the middle of the Crusades against Islam that preoccupied the kings and princes of Christendom for almost two centuries (1095 CE to 1291 CE). In the seven hundred twenty years since that human catastrophe, Christianity and Islam have become the two dominant religious communities of the modern world, sharing between them roughly one half of humanity. In our times, this land has become the scene of an epic struggle be-

Terrell E Arnold

tween millennium-old indigenous peoples and 20th century invaders who say they have prior rights. This land also has become the base of the world's fourth or fifth most heavily armed nuclear power: Israel. All of that has roots in a region at the eastern end of the Mediterranean that is now loosely referred to as Palestine.

The Place

As a place name Palestine came into more or less common usage beginning about 100 years ago. A variant spelling of the name was in use as early as 1500 years ago. The name translates from Arabic to English as "filastine" or "Philistine", which links it, at least etymologically, and probably historically, to people who inhabited the immediate region of Gaza about 1200 years before Christ. The warriors of ancient Egypt and Macedonia trampled it. Alexander transited it in search of power or adventure. The Ashkenazim Jewish Zionists—then in Europe—developed an interest in the region as early as the turn of the 20th century. Becoming a British mandate in 1923, it occupied a space surrounded by Egypt, the eastern end of the Mediterranean, Syria (a French Mandate), Iraq (a separate British Mandate), and Arabia, now the states of Kuwait, the Emirates, Saudi Arabia and Yemen. The British mandate map is shown below.

PALESTINE In Need of a Just God

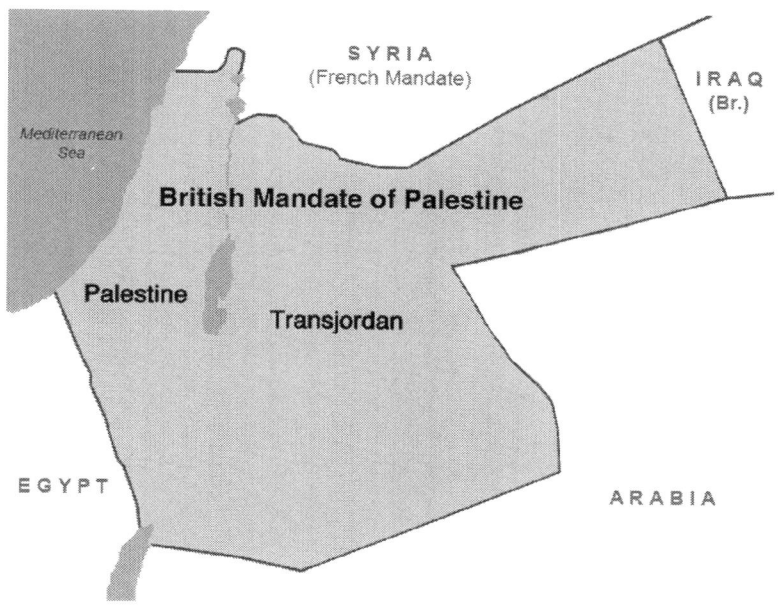

In the last era of the colonial empires, the British mandate of Palestine grew out of the division of the Middle East region among European colonial masters. They were engaged on both hastening and affirming the decline of the Ottoman Empire. While the formal British Mandate for Palestine was conferred by the League of Nations in 1923, the British had taken over earlier. The map of the Mandate appears to have been drawn by describing the boundaries of all the neighbors. There was no other map in common usage when the decision (the Balfour Declaration of 1917-Annex I) was made by Britain to *"view with favour the establishment in Palestine of a national home for the Jewish people"*.

Terrell E Arnold

With that background, the map of this land almost depends on who is drawing it and why. Zionist proponents of a Greater Israel (members of the European origin Ashkenazim Jewish community) wanted all of that territory and some of them still do.

The first map of significance to this discussion was presented by Zionist representatives to the Paris Peace Conference in 1919 (the conference that ended World War I). That map (see below) shows that Zionist ambitions for a Jewish national home were already well developed. Why it was presented, how it was argued, and what was done with the map are not available, but the map as superimposed on modern boundaries has a familiar look that resurfaced in the late 1940s. Note that future politically delicate areas such as (a) Lebanon south of the Litani River, (b) The Golan Heights of Syria, (c) the West Bank and Gaza Strip, (d) the lower basin of the Yarmuk River of what was then Transjordan and (e) the entire Jordan River are included inside the red line around the notional state of Israel.

PALESTINE In Need of a Just God

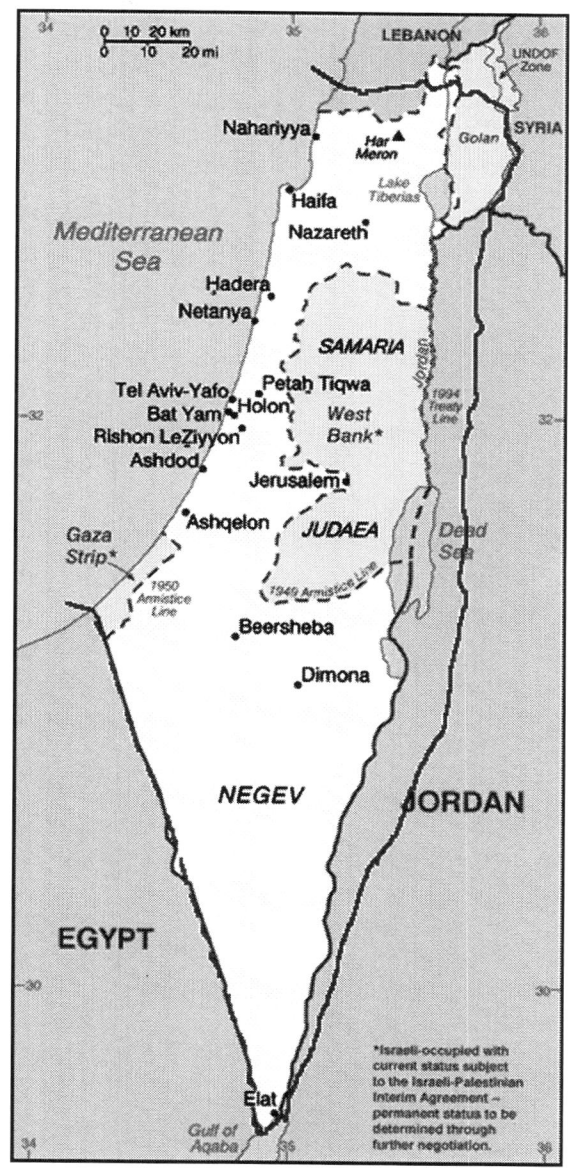

Terrell E Arnold

However, the land that actually was defined by the post-World War II UN decision to partition Palestine specified a single territory that was west of the Jordan River, south of modern Lebanon, west of a strip of Syria, west of Jordan, and northeast of Egypt. That real estate comprises the modern territory of Israel, the Gaza Strip and the West Bank of the Jordan River—all that is assigned in modern political geography to Palestine.

The territory of the Mandate east of the Jordan River was referred to by the British as Transjordan; it became a state (an emirate under the Mandate) in 1921, and the Jews coming into Palestine were forbidden by the British to migrate there. Jordan formally became the Hashemite Kingdom of Jordan in 1946, definitively closing off Zionist ambitions to make the region part of Greater Israel. Thus, by the time Israel declared its statehood in 1948, the area of Palestine had stabilized as shown in the map below. Even so, many Palestinians forced out of their homes went to Jordan.

PALESTINE In Need of a Just God

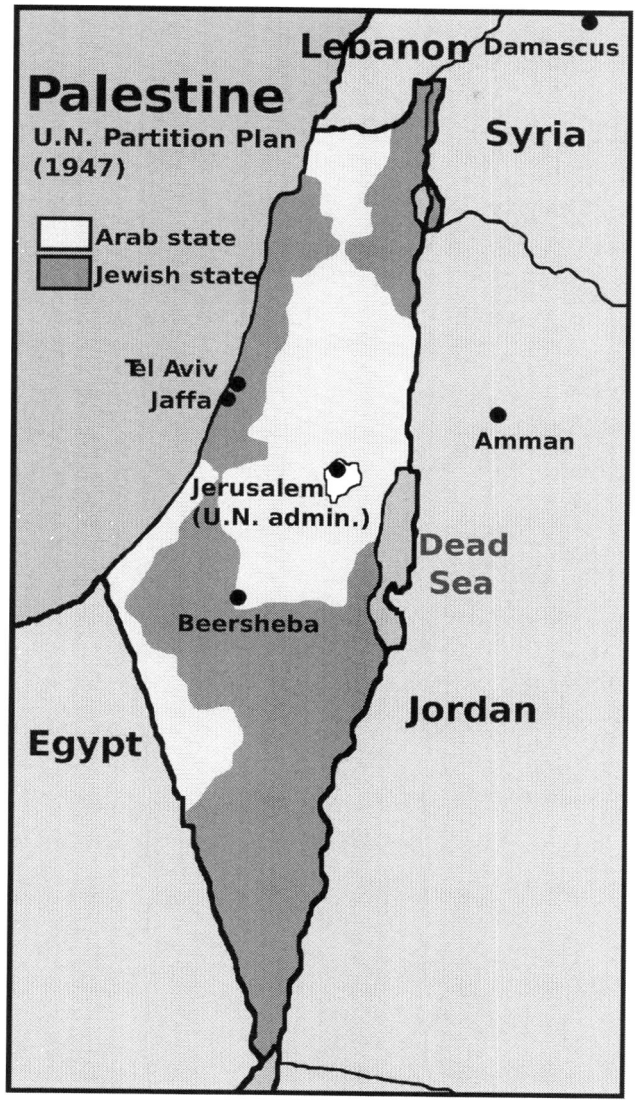

Terrell E Arnold

As the above map shows, the specific areas loosely assigned to Jews and Palestinians (Arabs on the map) under the UN partition plan were intermingled in an awkward pattern that basically assumed the Palestinians and Jews would have no choice but to live together. Students of that landscape say the best lands were given to the Israelis and the worst to the Palestinians. That issue aside, neither the Israelis nor the Palestinians ever subscribed to this map's living arrangements.

The modern map of Palestine, including Israel, has the same basic outline as the UN Partition map. Its eastern boundary is defined by the Jordan River, the Dead Sea, and the more or less straight but squiggly line that extends from the south edge of the Dead Sea to the upper end of the Gulf of Aqaba, as shown below. A quick flick of the eyes between the two maps will show readily the shrinkage of any area (highlighted as the West Bank and the Gaza Strip) the Israelis might concede to a Palestinian State.

PALESTINE In Need of a Just God

Terrell E Arnold

Not satisfied with that map, in the 1967—Six Day—War the Israelis occupied two other pieces of land that apparently they intend to keep. One is a piece of Lebanon called the Shebaa Farms. This arid area on the southeast side of Lebanon is bounded by the second piece of land, the Golan Heights, which Israel took from Syria. Israel has said it would like to keep both as a "security" protection, the Shebaa Farms to take maneuver room from the Lebanese insurgent group Hezbollah, and the Golan Heights as protection against possible invasion from Syria. Actually Israel values the Heights for tourist attractions, agricultural land and water resources. Both territories are now the subjects of unsettled disputes that, in principle, would be resolved by peace treaties between Israel and its northern neighbors, if and when they might occur.

Who Are the Palestinians?

Nailing down the people of the region by historic, ethnic, religious, or tribal connections is no simple matter. The region has been so long in the middle of the road between east and west, as well as north and south, that there is probably a bit of everything in its bloodstream. However, a significant element of the indigenous population has been on the landscape for centuries, in many cases millennia, and those are the people usually referred to as Palestinians. Their longevity on the site relates many of them to the "people of the book", the Semitic peoples, only some of whom were the Jews, who are referred to in the Bible. When the invasion of the

Ashkenazim Jews from Europe began after World War I, the indigenous population was about 800,000 people and consisted of Muslims (about 80%), Christians and non-believers (about 10%), and Jews (about 10%). Whatever their religious preferences, many of these people were descended from Shem, the legendary son of Abraham who sired the first of the Semitic peoples.

When the Zionist takeover got fully underway in 1947-48, there were more than a million Palestinians in the country. It was by no means an empty land—as advertised by the Zionists—and had not been empty from time immemorial. Under the pressures of Zionist ethnic cleansing—especially in coastal regions, most of the people were driven out of their ancestral homes and villages before 1967. The non-Jewish people scattered to the West Bank and Gaza regions, but many ended up in Jordan, Lebanon, Syria, Egypt, other surrounding countries, and various countries outside the region. Their homes and villages in Palestine were systematically destroyed by the Israelis to create a false image of Jewishness. Thus a process of conflict, expulsion, land confiscation, bloodshed, and pretense gave birth to the new state of Israel.

Despite the dispersion of many Palestinians into the outside world, by 2010 the resident Palestinian population had increased to roughly 1.5 million in the Gaza Strip, 2.5 million in the West Bank, and about 1.5 million inside Israel. The total Palestinian population of

Terrell E Arnold

about 5.5 million may be slightly smaller than the estimated Jewish population, but the Palestinians—with a more rapid birth rate—have been gaining on the Israelis and are expected to outnumber them in fairly short order. That prospect is referred to by many Israelis as their "demographic" crisis, a situation that is viewed by them as totally at odds with the idea of a "Jewish" national home. How could their home be Jewish if the non-Jewish population outnumbers the Jews?

The issues and choices surrounding this situation are openly and widely debated in Israel by the people and in the media. But the matter is not widely discussed anywhere else. Part of the trouble in this landscape lies with the fact that present day Israel's politically dominant Jewish population is derived from the European Ashkenazim group who descend from ethnic Turks, not Semites. Their origin is discussed below. The Sephardi, Mizrahi and other indigenous Jews of the region comprise a small majority of Jews in Israel. They are defined by origin or persuasion, meaning they are descended from the Sephardi Jews who were expelled from Spain in 1492, they are practitioners of Sephardi religious customs, or they are long term indigenous and regional Jews who are simply called Sephardi to distinguish them from the Ashkenazim. As late as the 1960s, Jews in Egypt and probably other North African countries still preserved 15th-century Spanish, the ancient tongue of the Sephardi, as a household language.

Who then are the Israelis of today?

The politically dominant Israelis are the Ashkenazim who are not Semitic or Middle Eastern in origin, but descend from the Central European Turkic tribe of the Khazars. The Khazars, who became the Ashkenazim, were a growing power in the Central European region when they decided that to maintain their independence in regional power games they needed to reject both Christianity and Islam. Thus they adopted Judaism. As Arthur Koestler describes the situation in his book, <u>The Thirteenth Tribe</u> (an engaging metaphor since the Khazars were not Semitic), the Khazars were once powerful in the region north of the Black Sea and the Caspian, a sizeable realm called Khazaria. They adopted Judaism in the 8th century, but their empire was wiped out by Genghis Khan, while the Khazars themselves "migrated to Poland and formed the cradle of Western (Ashkenazim) Jewry"...

The plan of the Ashkenazim to form a Jewish national home first surfaced sometime in the late 19th century, perhaps even earlier, and it may have been driven—at least in part—by memories of the loss of their Khazarian Empire. Zionism, belief in the nationalistic goal of forming a Jewish (Ashkenazim) national home, drove the politics of the movement. Several places (including African and Latin American) were considered for this home, but the one ultimately selected was Palestine because of its obvious linkage to the Jewish experience. As noted earlier, the Balfour Declaration that began lending substance to the plan was delivered in 1917. The whole World War II German and European experience of the Ashkenazim, including the Holocaust, served as a driver for implementing this plan, and as propaganda for promoting it, but the plan was well underway before World War II, and its origin was Ashkenazim Zionist ambition, not German repression. Early immigrants already had arrived in Palestine. Frictions already had begun to arise between the new settlers and the Palestinians. The future was apparent, if not ordained, well before World War II.

Unfortunately, it appears that the powerful Ashkenazim leadership, that ruled the new colony from the beginning, and has ruled it ever since the achievement of statehood, did not think highly of the indigenous population of Palestine. They looked down on the Sephardi Jews as well as non-Jews in the regional population. In this sense, Israeli democracy got off to a start that was actually quite racially charged, and it still struggles with that problem. Critics of the plan for the all-Jewish state asserted virtually from the beginning that the idea was blatantly racist. That certainly appears so, but the dominant racial preference actually continues to be for the Ashkenazim and their offspring, more than for the sons and daughters of Shem.

Who are the present Palestinians?

Despite their troubled 20th-century history, and their repressed circumstances, the Palestinians have

PALESTINE In Need of a Just God

emerged as an interesting, dynamic and talented society. Slowly but surely, under a brutal and unpredictable Israeli occupation for the past four decades, they have developed the capabilities and institutions to govern themselves, to provide up through university levels of education, to master modern technologies, and to provide public services that are limited only by their repressed status under the Israeli occupation. That they have achieved so much despite over six decades of uncertainty, harassment, displacement, killing, and military occupation is a marvel in its own right. Meanwhile, the rest of the world has benefitted from the large Palestinian diaspora, because there are talented Palestinians in key areas of public life in many countries as well as the United Nations.

A Bit of History

While the combination of Israel, Gaza and the West Bank covers a small area, in ancient times the region harbored many even smaller kingdoms, as shown below. That map suggests that by the time of Christ the region was already a complex socio-religious region that probably has retained elements of that experience across the intervening centuries. Place names, especially coastal cities are pretty much still intact. The mind of the young Jesus was exposed to many cultures and beliefs.

Terrell E Arnold

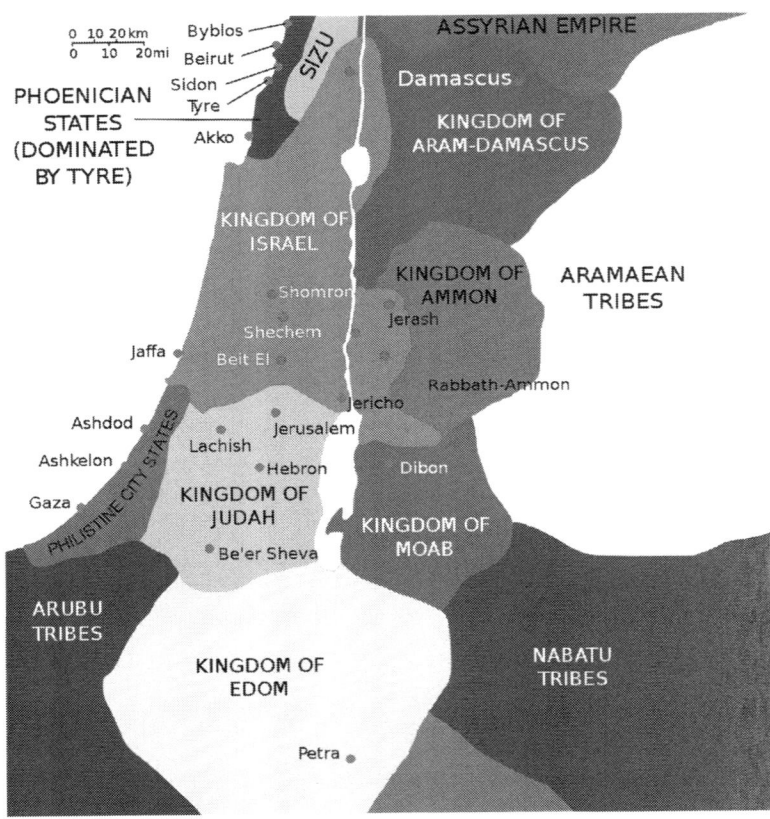

The region about 830 BCE

Although Palestine as a place has been around for centuries, the Palestinian people reportedly came together in the period beginning around 1830 when the Egyptians under Mohammed Ali took over forceful rule of the territory from Ottoman Turkey. The troops of Mohammed Ali set out to pacify the region and they took on three of the four main provinces of Palestine (Galilee, Samaria, Judah). They seem to have left people in the desert region of the Negeb (Negev) alone. While the people of those provinces had comparatively little to do with each other in any administrative sense, the emergence of a common enemy appears to have brought them together.

The Egyptian forces were better trained, equipped and supplied, but the Palestinians outnumbered them, knew the territory better, engaged in effective guerilla warfare, and made life uncertain if not miserable for the Egyptian troops. Recapturing the territory in 1840, Ottoman rulers found the Palestinians had more or less come together into a single population. They have stayed together pretty much ever since, but the unifying force for much of the past century has been the Israeli Zionist enemy whose Ashkenazim leadership seeks not merely to rule Palestine but to expel the Palestinian people from their homeland. Various invaders have ruled, repressed and abused the Palestinians, but so far only the Israelis have sought to erase them from their homeland altogether.

The Present Situation

Honing of the Palestinian personality continues into the present era. The recent fly in this ointment, from US, Israeli and the Palestinian Fatah political party points of view, has been the maturity of the Islamic insurgent group Hamas into an effective and electorally

Terrell E Arnold

successful political party. While the US and Israel promoted the 2006 Palestinian People's Assembly elections as a way of supporting Yasser Arafat's old Fatah party and his successor Mahmoud Abbas (PLO/war name: Abu Mazen), they were rudely shocked by the outcome. Hamas won a strong Assembly majority; meaning it was able to form a government without help.

The US and Israel have led in refusing to accept the political victories of Hamas. They have refused to do business with a Hamas-led government, sticking to their repeated vigorous assertions that Hamas is merely a terrorist group.

That position is narrowly and strictly Israeli and Zionist self-serving, because it derives from their recognition that Hamas stands for the basic Palestinian political agenda. While the Hamas charter calls for the destruction of Israel, their current agenda is more modest and is widely shared by Palestinians. As specified in the Arab League proposal that emerged from the League's 2002 meeting in Beirut, that agenda calls for: (a) A Palestinian state based on the 1949 green-truce/1967 cease-fire-line boundaries (the green line because it was drawn on the map in green ink) with adjustments by mutual consent, (b) a right of return and/or (c) compensation for property confiscated by the Israelis, and (d) a capital in East Jerusalem. Fatah has been pushed repeatedly by Israel to bargain on those objectives and some say they may have given away much of the store, but there is actually very little binding documentation. In any case, the

Israelis so far have given nothing in return for Palestinian concessions.

For its work throughout Palestinian territory, Hamas has the reputation as an able and honest public administrator. However, its political strength probably derives mostly from its firm position on the key Palestinian homeland issues cited above.

Inability to get Hamas and Fatah together on governance has stalled real Palestinian leadership development and political evolution for at least the past five years. In fact, Mahmoud Abbas and the Fatah party have been actively supported by the US and Israel in efforts to keep Hamas out of Palestinian governance. Possibly breaking out of that box, initial steps were taken by Fatah and Hamas in early May 2011 to form a unity government. While it was tried about five years before and even more recently but failed, a unity government long has been the objective of Hamas. On the other hand, Fatah has sought to suppress political opposition. Fatah as well as Mahmoud Abbas have had the help of the US and Israel in trying to minimize the impact of Hamas popularity. But their attitudes and maneuvers appear only to have strengthened Hamas among the Palestinian people and among Arab as well as other countries.

Aside from facing Israel and the US with a need to decide how they will deal with whoever will run Palestine, the successful development of a unity government has the potential to force the issue on how the final map of Israel and Palestine will look, as well as how much real control the US and Israel would have over it. Rather less forcefully than he might have, President Obama has come out in favor of a two-state solution with an Israeli-Palestinian state boundary based on the 1967 ceasefire line with swaps for Palestinians to regain land lost to settlements.

That line actually represented the line agreed among Israel, Jordan, Egypt and Syria at the end of the 1949 Middle East war. While remaining informal, it became the boundary of territory annexed by Jordan's King Abdullah in the1956 war; and as the 1967 ceasefire line it has also come to describe the line between Israel and the territory of the West Bank. In principle, this line would demark the boundary between the State of Israel and the State of Palestine. However, Benyamin Netanyahu's hard right and largely Ashkenazim government objects strongly to any consideration of that line because it would force Israel territorially to define its boundaries by making room for Palestine.

Thus the 1949 green line/1967 ceasefire line became the long-term notional boundary of Israel, even though no Israeli government ever formally subscribed to it. In fact, in recent years the Israelis have tinkered with that line with their meandering wall, with an Israeli-only road system in the West Bank (on confiscated land), and with officially supported West Bank settler developments—also Israeli land theft from the Palestinians. Moreover, in a letter to Ariel Sharon in 2004, then

PALESTINE In Need of a Just God

President George W. Bush essentially adopted Israeli settler confiscation of lands in the West Bank (that is beyond the green line) as what he called "facts on the ground." (See Bush letter at Annex II)

That the United States actually has any legal authority to give Palestinian land to the Israelis seems highly unlikely and has been questioned by several people. However, the Bush position follows a pattern of high-level US assertions that become in practical effect US policy underwriting of Israeli land grabs that violate Palestinian rights and international law.

Ironically, one might observe that Bush probably had as much authority as Lord Balfour who gave the would-be state of Israel land that at the time belonged to Turkey. Having occupied the area in the 1967 War, while it is illegal under international law to acquire territory by force, it looks as if the Israelis could be allowed to get away with it, at least so long as their ally is the United States.

That indeed is the core problem of making peace in the Holy Land. Israel is allowed to make its own rules. However, the Palestinians, under occupation, are supposed to do what they are told. That situation, of course, would change if Palestine succeeds in its September 2011 UN General Assembly bid to gain entry or recognition as a nation state. It would become the 194th member of the United Nations. Already 120 members of the UN, including ten members of the Security Council, have recognized the state of Palestine.

Until the UN acts, Israel is likely to go on ignoring that pattern of recognition. But UN acceptance would require Israel to deal with Palestine as an equal. The new State of Palestine would have rights and privileges equal to any other nation state.

Meanwhile, Israel continues to grab more land. Israeli leadership professes to need control of the Jordan River Valley as a security measure. In reality, Jordan probably needs such a buffer more than Israel. However, with that move, Israel would literally surround any Palestinian state and could absolutely control its future as a slave state that could do nothing without Israeli approval.

In fact, there is no evidence of any threat from Jordan. Rather the real reason for control of the upper and lower Jordan valley (the so-called Ghor—upper- and Zor—lower valley) is to reserve control to the Israelis while denying any control of Jordan River water and related aquifers to the Palestinians. This has been a long-standing concern of the Palestinians, and it will become an issue for hard bargaining in final Palestinian state building. How hard will significantly be determined by how well the Palestinian statehood declaration is received by the UN and its membership in September.

PALESTINE In Need of a Just God

Except for the Sabras (the new native Israelis) who have been born in Israel since the invasion began, the Ashkenazim have no real Palestinian roots. Their takeover of Palestine is an outsider's power and political game, not the return of a lost tribe. Their invasion and occupation of Palestine would be rigorously opposed by the whole world if the invader were virtually any other national or religious group. The symbolism of it looks increasingly false as Israel's Zionist adherents endeavor to raze the indigenous history of the region and implant a contrived invader one. At best that is an imported racist model that holds no promise for the Palestinian people.

In the end, however, it would be just, as well as human, for the Palestinian people to have a big part of their homeland and be able to continue the evolving history of the Palestinian people in Palestine. That is what they hope to nail down by going to the UN for recognition as the State of Palestine. It is to be hoped that dealing with the Israelis as equals will assure that Palestinians retain their base and their self-respect in the land of their birth.

The following articles dealing with the situation of the Palestinian people and with their struggle to survive were written over a period of nearly six years and published on the Internet site rense.com on the dates cited at the top of each article. Various sources and individuals have been consulted and drawn upon over the years. However, the views and opinions expressed here are entirely those of the author.

Chapter 2.
Clueless In Gaza

9-18-05

Since the death of Yasser Arafat in November 2004, the Middle East peace process has been on a dual track. One track is apparent motion called the "peace process" that always falls short of progress. The other is real movement toward chaos and continued Israeli efforts to extinguish Palestinian rights. Reading the signs of these two concurrent motions is sometimes like interpreting tea leaves, but recent events reveal a hardening reality.

Israeli Prime Minister Ariel Sharon added a strange warp to the situation with his address to the United Nations General Assembly on Wednesday (September 14). Not generally well-received there, this time he spellbound his audience. "The Palestinians", he said, "will always be our neighbors. We respect them and don't aspire to rule over them. They also deserve freedom and a sovereign national entity in their own country." All of those widely held truths were uttered by the man who has done more than most other individual Israelis to liquidate or dispossess and expel the Palestinian people from Israel, the West Bank, and Gaza. Reflecting the amazement generated by Sharon's pronouncement, no delegation walked out of the Assembly session except Iran.

Reactions to this bombshell were all over the map. Benyamine Netanyahu, who sees himself as Sharon's successor, accused Sharon of totally abandoning his "roots". Sharon was further accused of moving to the extreme left and joining the peace camp. But Palestinians saw nothing of substance in the statement, and immediately subsequent events surely proved them right.

In a statement hardly more than travel time and distance away from his UN address, Sharon repudiated his UN General Assembly statements. As reported by witnesses, he told an academic group in northern Israel that he rejected Israeli withdrawal to the 1967 borders—the so-called "green line"; he rejected the idea of any Palestinian capital in East Jerusalem; and he opposed any right of return for Palestinians. Sharon also said that his position was accepted by the United States. As previously mentioned, last year George W. Bush wrote a politically well-timed letter to that effect to Sharon. (See Annex II) The letter was blessed by a Congressional resolution. (See annex IV).

Meanwhile, Mahmoud Abbas and the Palestine Authority are moving toward an election to be held early next year, and they are struggling to tame their "extremists": Hamas, the al Aqsa Martyrs Brigades, Palestine Islamic Jihad and three or four other groups. The Authority has three choices:

(1) Leave them as spoilers outside the peace process and cope with the effects of their violence against the Israelis;

(2) Encourage them to put down their weapons and join the political process; or

(3) Eliminate or neutralize them.

Sharon and Israel's Likud (the political party Sharon leads), as well as others concerned about suicide bombers and stray missiles, have made any peace agreement contingent on shutting down the violence. While Israelis generally have not dictated to the Palestinians how they should do that, Likud leaders have always pursued solution number three.

Any realistic observer of the Middle East situation knows that the first solution is not tolerable, and the third is not doable even though the Israelis continue to persecute the Palestinian people. That leaves the middle ground, and that is where Mahmoud Abbas and his team have been trying to move the outcome, with the upcoming January 2006 People's Assembly elections as the first opportunity to bring the extremists in from the cold.

The task is not simple. No Palestinian groups trust either the Israelis or the United States. Some of them have numerous problems, e.g., with arrests of group members, and with the incompetence and corruption within the Palestine Authority.

Further complicating this landscape, reportedly Israelis fear that if Hamas were to field candidates they could garner 40% of the vote in Gaza and perhaps the West Bank. Such a vote would demonstrate that there remains great nervousness and/or strong opposition among Palestinians to any peace deal so far offered. The kinds of proposals that have been floated in the past by the Israelis and blessed more or less automatically by the United States and others simply have no standing with these groups. Nor do those proposals stand up in the face of growing Israeli settlements and the intrusive wall in the West Bank, despite the Israeli withdrawal from Gaza. Sharon's recent statements to academics cited above can only harden such objections.

Sharon himself seems bent on making the cheese more binding. According to The New York Times, Sharon met with journalists in New York on Friday (September 16) and took a categorical position. If Hamas fields candidates, Sharon said "we will make every effort not to help them." He then cited actual obstructions to any Palestinian election by suggesting that roadblocks and checkpoints would not be removed, thereby actively interfering with the vote. With these statements, Sharon has made crystal clear what was obvious in the last election: Elections in Palestine are fine, so long as the candidates are approved by the Israelis, and of course by the United States.

PALESTINE In Need of a Just God

As reported in The New York Times, a spokesman for the US National Security Council went even further. He declared that "Hamas is a terrorist group" which is actually not in dispute, although insurgent group appears more accurate; he then reiterated the long-standing US position against talking to terrorists but added a twist: "We will not talk to any elected officials who are members of a terrorist group." With that in mind, one can muse over the number of former Israeli Stern, Irgun or Haganah terrorists who have been elected to public office and received at the White House, including Sharon, Begin and Shamir, all of whom appear to have remained barely reconstructed.

It is obvious that Mahmoud Abbas and the Palestinian Authority cannot move forward without the insurgents in the van. They must somehow be brought on board or no Palestinian government and certainly no peace agreement with Israel would be stable, even if it were possible. The Palestinians already know that candidate selection in the previous election was rigged. Had it not been, the most likely candidate, Marwan Barghouti, the founding leader of the al Aqsa Brigades who continues to reside in an Israeli prison, may well have won hands down. But he and al Aqsa, like Hamas and the other groups, stand on the wrong side. He and they are simply not likely to accept the slippery and substantively deferred kinds of Israeli promises they have heard many times before.

Terrell E Arnold

The tragedy is that the Israelis and the United States are forcing the Palestinian leadership situation into its worst possible form. That assures some pattern of continuing attacks against Israel, sustains a continuing Israeli occupation in the West Bank, and makes it likely that peace simply is not attainable. It has been said that Sharon needs the Palestinian terrorism to keep his game going. That may not be literally true, but he certainly has been working hard this week to make it so. This has to be deliberate, or we must assume that both Sharon and the Bush team are wandering clueless in Gaza.

Chapter 3.
Time To Grow Up

1-28-06

This week the Palestinian insurgent group Hamas exceeded predictions for its political debut by winning an absolute majority in the Palestinian People's Assembly. Not only did it sweep Fatah strongholds such as Ramallah; it also won in Bethlehem and Jerusalem where the Israelis refused to allow Hamas candidates to campaign. The victories did not happen because Hamas had acquired political skill without even practicing. They happened because Palestinians were demanding change; because Ariel Sharon and his supporters had worked unceasingly to keep Arafat and his successor Mahmoud Abbas from ever succeeding; because anyone watching the so-called "peace process" on the ground knew it was going nowhere.

Hamas leadership may have been as surprised as anyone that they won the elections. However, for several months local reports have suggested that a new kind of reality was descending on Palestine. Young Palestinians, even within Fatah, were fed up with the old guard. They were unhappy about Fatah cronyism, about the millions of dollars—provided by various donors to the Palestinian people—that had disappeared into private coffers of the Fatah inner circle. They were fed up with the political bankruptcy, the moral and monetary corruption of Fatah. Start with the fact that before his death Arafat may have been virtually under house arrest in Ramallah, but his wife lived in luxury in Paris. Abbas, known by his PLO-Fatah name as Abu Mazen, himself apparently occupies a house in Gaza that cost over a million dollars to build. These odious comparisons are not lost on ordinary Palestinians.

The reality is that a time for change in Palestinian leadership truly had come. Abu Mazen had failed to transform Palestinian leadership after the death of Yasser Arafat. He failed not because he was weak or incompetent, but because he had no help. Bush applauded him as a head of state on his visit to the United States, but Bush continued to deliver total support to his friend, Ariel Sharon, on all issues that mattered to the Palestinian people. Sharon did everything he could to assure Abu Mazen's failure, including construction of new settlements, continued building of the wall, targeted assassinations of Palestinian insurgent leaders, and continuing, often brutish, occupation of Palestinian territory. All of those factors have contributed to a realistic Palestinian sense that Fatah can do nothing for them.

The question now is where do things go from here? The Bush administration has averred it will not work with Hamas in the government. Secretary of State Rice has said she will continue to work with Abu Mazen; that, in a narrow sense, is correct, because he has three more

PALESTINE In Need of a Just God

years of his term as President. But how will he be able to work with a Hamas-led parliament? The Israelis have said they will not negotiate with a Hamas government. The New York Times suggests the Israelis will respond by increasingly unilateral action, although how that will differ from what they have been doing for years—building the wall, confiscating Palestinian lands, building new settlements, hogging available water, and killing Palestinian insurgents—is not clear. Europeans do not appear overjoyed by the prospect, but they have not been so categorical in reaction. Middle Eastern supporters of the Palestinian Intifada are jubilant. Everybody has to wait for real indications of what Hamas might do with its opportunity for leadership.

Meanwhile the Bush administration assertion that it will not work with terrorists poses some challenging problems. As Secretary Rice has put it, Hamas cannot "have one foot in politics and the other in terror." That posture may have standing as an expression of the US policy of "no concessions to terrorists". However, it ignores the reality of the change in Hamas political standing; Abu Mazen has no choice but to recognize the Hamas parliamentary victory. He knows that and has asked Hamas to form a new government. Outsiders, whoever they may be, actually have no real choice but to recognize the change in Palestinian political reality: Its leading insurgency has won a political victory.

The smart choice would be to help Abu Mazen walk Hamas through the transition from insurgency to political party. The alternative is to continue trying to prevent Hamas from reacting to the persistent pattern of Israeli provocation. Efforts of outsiders to suppress or ignore Hamas will almost certainly retard any conversion.

The thing about insurgents is that, if they are successful, they are unlikely to arrive at the political table with clean hands. The IRA until recently had been an enduring bad example. In his youth Ariel Sharon, along with other founding Israeli politicians, was a terrorist with the blood of many Palestinian villagers on his hands. Their transition was easy because outsiders, especially the US, did not hold them to account.

In the past two days both the President and the Congress have expressed a typical knee-jerk US alliance with the Israelis on refusing to accept Hamas as a political player. Thus, the US appears unlikely to extend much considered acceptance of political growth by the Palestinians. Yet it is in everybody's interest to make the effort.

Hamas is already showing signs that it knows this is a new ball game. It is also a new ball game for the US, Israel, the Europeans, and numerous Arab supporters of the Palestinian people. Failure to recognize that and to accommodate the likely changes that are needed will assuredly lead to more violence, and even a successful transition may not occur without incident.

PALESTINE In Need of a Just God

After an intensive and politically disruptive effort to suppress the Sandinistas in Nicaragua, the US had to accept, if not admit defeat. The Sandinistas quite successfully made the transition to political maturity, but there remains an enduring trail of bitterness. They also transformed Nicaraguan political leadership without US help, but after the collapse of the US-supported Contras, they were not threatened by the neighbors.

No matter what they do, the Palestinians face a hostile neighbor and a continuing prospect of conflict and attrition from the Israelis, many of whom want all the rest of Biblical Palestine. The US has signed on to that Israeli agenda, perhaps explicitly; the Bush letter to Sharon was endorsed by the Congress. Hamas, therefore, will have to be shown proofs to expect any positive gesture from the United States. In that respect, the administration is not off to a good start with its public rejection of a political Hamas.

If not a transition to Hamas, then some other, equally profound change had to occur in Palestine. Under Arafat, Fatah had pretty well suppressed any evolutionary political succession. Abbas may be too much a part of that history to lead the way. The sustained lack of orderly political evolution portended either collapse or abrupt change, but the change is not as abrupt as it may seem.

Hamas has been far more useful than the names usually pinned on it—insurgent, terrorist, or Islamic extremist—would imply. For the better part of two decades Hamas has responded effectively to the economic and social needs of many Palestinians. In the districts where it was politically successful, meaning most of the West Bank as well as Gaza, people have looked to Hamas for human level support (welfare, security, food, medicine, and defense). In fact, Hamas has been the only domestic official organization effectively to provide these services in Palestine, even including creation and support for a thoroughly modern hospital in the Gaza Strip. Unspecified Arab donors have made this possible, and no doubt for many Palestinians, Hamas provision of such services has been a constant reminder of the incompetence and decay of Fatah and the Palestinian Authority.

Now that Hamas has won an election, the key to this situation is its transitional nature. That is potentially dangerous in two senses. If Hamas is not assisted and encouraged through the transit to full political maturity, if it is rejected as the legitimate voice of a large segment of the Palestinian people, it can easily be provoked to regroup around its insurgent personality and return to violence. To be sure, it has not yet rejected violence altogether—that, to be realistic about an occupied Palestine, is part of the Hamas political appeal.

By running successfully for political office Hamas has started down a non-violent path. Failure to encourage it further in this direction will be a foolish move on everybody's part. At the same time, if the people who voted for Hamas are disappointed by rejection of what they think is a promising political development, any reversion to insurgency by Hamas will be reinforced by new recruits and new sources of support.

This prospect actually gives the Israelis, the US, and other interested outsiders two choices: (a) Help the new generation of Palestinian politicians, including Hamas, through this process of change, or (b) reject the change and invite the bloody consequences of failure. Unless the goal is unending warfare, it is time to think about how to make this work.

There is no question that Hamas poses an unwanted challenge for some. Too bad. It is time we grew up. Don't tout the virtues of democracy if you are not prepared to live with the results. Several countries of Latin America are rubbing our noses in that lesson. The dominant political results in Iraq have delivered the same message: Given a choice, the Iraqis voted their ethnic and religious preferences, despite the secularizing changes Saddam had introduced in his long rule.

People in a democracy are free to decide who will rule them. In many cases, that may not be the people we would like to see elected. Hamas challenges us to have the courage of our own democratic convictions. The alternative is regime change imposed by outsiders, which, of course, is undemocratic and contrary to international law.

Chapter 4.
Collective Punishment Is Wrong

2-5-06

In its first election try last week, the Palestinian insurgent group Hamas won the majority of seats in the Palestinian People's Assembly. Prior to this election campaign Hamas and its followers had held themselves aloof from politics, asserting that the politicians, mainly in Fatah, were corrupt, inept and unable to resist the occupation, land theft and harassment by the Israelis. Meanwhile, as it continued to resist Israeli occupation, Hamas became the most effective provider of human services in Palestine. Other insurgencies—e.g., the Sandinistas in Nicaragua or the Moro National Liberation Front in the Philippines—have had to do some of that to be convincing, but none has equaled the back door political maturation of Hamas through organized public service.

Outside of NGOs actively working in Palestine, the public service side of Hamas has gone virtually unnoticed, certainly unheralded. That is because the western media and political mantra for Hamas is "Islamic extremist terrorist group". Public service does not make headlines, but lobbing a mortar shell from the Gaza Strip into an Israeli street does, especially if people are harmed. The fact that it is the right of any determined individual to resist the presence of an invading army is ignored in this case. An invading Israeli army can destroy homes, towns, the Palestinian infrastructure in pursuit of suspected militants and that is OK, but fighting back is not. "Collateral damage" to innocent bystanders, including women and children is an unfortunate product of Israeli warfare in Palestinian territory, but Palestinian attacks against their oppressors in Israeli territory are labeled terrorism, not warfare.

This harsh double standard is among the reasons Hamas has avoided the political process up to now. Even before the occupation, the Israelis practiced "targeted assassinations" and other attacks on Palestinians in the West Bank and Gaza. But those attacks were justified in the West, especially in the United States, as Israel's right to defend itself. At no time was it ever conceded that the Palestinians, e.g., Hamas, the al Aqsa Brigades, or other Palestinian resistance groups, had any right to defend themselves or their homes or their communities.

This dichotomy has been rigorously observed in Israeli and US official positions. It was unlikely to be questioned so long as the resistance groups had no political standing. Last week's election changed the situation, both for Hamas and for its critics.

PALESTINE In Need of a Just God

The struggle of Israel and the west to digest the Hamas People's Assembly victory in Palestine has moved the US, the UN, the European Union and Russia—the Quartet concerned with Middle East peace talks—to assertive bargaining by pronouncement. After a meeting on Monday (May 1) with the Quartet, UN Secretary General Kofi Annan sided with the US on cutting aid to the Palestinians because of Hamas. Britain's Jack Straw, the French PM and Germany's new Chancellor, Angela Merkel, voiced similar sentiments. Basically Annan said that any Hamas government would have to recognize Israel's right to exist and renounce violence. Aid to Palestine, he said, "would be reviewed by donors" with an eye to assuring Palestinian compliance with such requirements. On that basis, aid would be withheld from all Palestinians, even those who voted for Fatah and other parties, unless Hamas met those commitments with others contained in the Road Map drawn up by the Quartet to shape peace negotiations.

This week Jordan and Egypt voiced the accepted litany, saying they would not do business with Hamas unless it renounced violence and recognized Israel. Egypt went so far as to suggest that Abu Mazen form a government with the minority parties, that is leave the majority party out of the new Palestinian government. This position was taken no doubt as a result of heavy US and Israeli pressure.

Meanwhile, the US Congress has gotten into the act, A Senate resolution sponsored by Senator John

Terrell E Arnold

Thune of South Dakota provides: "it is the sense of Congress that no United States assistance should be provided to the Palestinian Authority if any representative political party holding a majority of parliamentary seats within the Palestinian Authority maintains a position calling for the destruction of Israel."

The Palestinian Democracy Support Act, introduced in the House by automatically pro-Israel Representative Tom Lantos of California and similarly committed Representative Ileana Ros-Lehtinen of Florida provides that if the Palestinians do not carry out a litany of eight or more actions this law would end US assistance: prohibit Palestinian diplomats from entering the US; designate Palestine as a terrorist sanctuary; and reduce US contributions to the UN by the same percentage that UN money is spent on Palestine. A second House bill introduced by Representative Vito Fossella of New York would also cut aid to Palestine.

This is an outburst of indignation that neither Washington nor, for that matter, European governments are likely to mount on their own. They only could or would mount such a flurry under the political lash of Israeli outrage. But behind that outrage is obviously a fear that the Palestinian election might just have to be taken seriously. That means such things as the hardline Hamas stand against Israel, which has been known for decades, now must be addressed. Others might hope that all involved might also search out why that hardline position exists.

PALESTINE In Need of a Just God

While western governments and the UN are threatening to reduce aid, the Israelis are indicating that they may withhold customs duties that have been paid by Palestinians and are due to the Palestinian Authority. The Israelis act as tax collector for the Palestinians and collect revenues amounting to about $50 million per month. They have withheld these revenues before as a blackmail tool.

But what would be different about a government that includes Hamas? Palestinian insurgent groups have always been suspicious and distrustful of the peace process. That process generally has involved a proposed trade of immediate Palestinian concessions for promises of equally painful but future Israeli ones. Arafat was less and less able to make any headway in negotiations as that lopsided trading pattern became obvious to more and more Palestinians and their Arab backers. What Hamas saw was a peace process that led only to talking and still more talking while the Israelis continued to annex new territory. The Hamas strategy has been to seek real and present concessions from Israel for real and present concessions from Palestine.

Hamas has maintained that posture while continuing to carry and, from time to time, to use the insurgent stick. That posture obviously had more appeal to Palestinian voters last week than the lackluster negotiating performance of Fatah. But the western reaction and now the reactions of all of Palestine's neighbors except

Syria are to find ways to suppress the results of the Palestinian election.

President Bush put the last nail in the Palestinian election coffin before and during the State of the Union Tuesday night when he said the US will not support a Hamas government unless it gives up its arms and recognizes Israel. This posture supports the long term Israeli negotiating practice of extracting present Palestinian concessions without any Israeli quid pro quo. All of the heat is on Palestine.

Meanwhile, Hamas leadership is proceeding very carefully. Some Hamas voices are speaking out, but the organization is basically keeping its head down. It is useful in this context to review just where Hamas has stood in the past. Since the election, Hamas spokesmen have begun a process of (a) reminding people where Hamas has stood for years on the leading issues, and (b) of subtly laying a negotiating strategy on the table for interested parties to view. As indicated by one Hamas interpreter, "Hamas will end violence but keep the Dream."

The elements of the dream were probably first outlined by the late leader of Hamas, Sheikh Ahmad Yassin, who was deliberately killed several years ago by an Israeli air to surface missile. Yassin said that the Palestinians (a) would never recognize the theft of their land, but (b) they were willing to negotiate a cease-fire, even one that could last for a generation. In exchange, (c) Israel would have to give back "what it occupied in 1967"—

meaning move back to the green armistice line. That would mean give up all settlements in the West Bank and Gaza (the latter already having been done). A final condition would require Israel to release all Palestinian prisoners, now numbering more than 9,000 individuals.

Those prisoners include the most popular Fatah political figure, Marwan Barghouti, who is now serving five consecutive life sentences in an Israeli prison for crimes hardly as horrendous as those for which Sharon and other Israeli terrorists never even went to jail. While no one can speak for him, as founder of the insurgent al Aqsa Brigades he would quite likely side with Hamas.

As anyone who has worked on the issues knows, such an agenda, if put forward by Hamas, would involve enormous concessions by the Palestinians as well. It would grant the existence of Israel. But it would not forgive the very large bill for Israeli confiscated Palestinian property. The Palestinians have claims for property that could cover hundreds of villages ravaged since the late 1940s. New settlements built on confiscated Palestinian land continue to add to that bill. The enormity of these property claims may well be a principal driver of Israeli efforts to make the Palestinians go away without a struggle.

It is important and urgent for all the agitated critics of Hamas and the election outcome to note that the Hamas charter, which has defined its recruitment effort and graphically defined Palestine's enemy, does not appear in its negotiating demands. What does appear clear in the Hamas posture is it is time to stop temporizing. It is time to recognize that a stalled "peace process" has been systematically used by the Israelis to maintain a conflict that provides cover while they slowly but surely absorb the West Bank.

That tactic is at once a provocation and an everyday preoccupation to the Palestinians. It must stop. It is time for all those who are now dancing around in indignation over the election of Hamas to begin looking candidly at the mounting crimes of the Israelis against the Palestinian people. That means at the least that some sense of fairness must come into play here. Hamas won the election because Palestinians had concluded that Fatah was totally bankrupt, while Hamas, in sharp contrast, seemed capable in Palestinian eyes of doing something about those problems.

Much has been made in western media about the so-called peace process. However, that process has been celebrated more by outsiders than by the Palestinian people. On the day after the election they had real cause to be proud of themselves. Bringing the main insurgent group into the political process was a major step forward. If the outside world succeeds in suppressing this first real breakthrough in the Palestinian configuration for peace, the burden of guilt will be on them, not on Hamas, and not on the Palestinian people.

PALESTINE In Need of a Just God

Ultimately it is time for outsiders to stop telling a newly elected political party what it must do to take office. What it must do—under the rules of democracy—is respond to the needs of its constituency. Hamas made the first move in the right direction when it put its members forward as candidates in a democratic election. If the leadership of Hamas has not yet understood how large a problem it faces, it will soon know in spades how tricky it is to transit from insurgency to governance.

How Hamas may govern and respond to its foreign policy needs, including relations with Israel, cannot be determined in advance. It certainly should not be determined by western and Israeli dictate. Nor should the Hamas posture be changed without real Israeli concessions. All outstanding matters, including the Hamas posture, are proper issues for bargaining, but Palestine needs its new government—and time—to do that.

Whatever message the very well mobilized supporters of Israel may have hoped to deliver, the Palestinians must not be told they cannot decide for themselves who will govern them. It is therefore time for all the critics to back off and give the Palestinian people room. It was by all accounts a fair and open election. They should be applauded, not punished for it.

Chapter 5.
The Recognition Stumbling Block

2-13-06

"Hamas has arrived at the doors of power through legitimate elections," said Russian President Putin last Thursday during a joint press conference with the Prime Minister of Spain. He said that Russia does not consider Hamas a terrorist organization. Moreover, he declared that Russia would invite Hamas representatives to come to Moscow for talks in the future. That presumably would be under Russia's role in the Quartet with the United States, the UN, and the European Union that is responsible for navigating the Road Map to Middle East peace. On Friday France indicated that it supported the Putin plan to invite Hamas to Moscow.

Israeli officials uniformly have loudly protested the Putin invitation, asserting that it threatens peace prospects. Israelis have been trying to have all governments shun Hamas because its charter called for destruction of Israel. Calling the Putin invitation a "slap in the face" to Israel and to western countries, Israelis said it was Russia's responsibility to shun Hamas.

However, according to the New York Times, a French Foreign Ministry spokesman stated that "We share with Russia the goal of leading Hamas toward positions that permit reaching the objective of two states living in peace and security."

Putin's statements indicated plainly that Russia has moved to the next square concerning Palestinian politics and Middle East peace. Putin appeared unmoved by Israeli protests, or by the probable—behind the scenes—efforts others have made to make him change his mind.

Out of obeisance to Israel, the West struggles pretty uniformly to figure out what to do about the Hamas political victory in Palestine. Putin has seen both the reality and the opportunity. He suddenly is in at least a metaphorical class—one he may not even recall—with Harry Truman, who was the first to recognize the fledgling self-declared state of Israel in 1948. France, less closely tied to US positions than most Europeans, basically followed suit by supporting the Russian position.

Hamas, ready or not, entered the forever dicey realm of great power competition for present and future influence, if not pre-eminence in the Middle East. However it plays out, the pending visit to Moscow is a very important moment for Hamas.

It will be, most likely, the first Hamas toe in the tricky waters of Middle East peace negotiations. When they are in Russia, as Putin statements already have indicated, the Hamas representatives will be pressed on the need to recognize Israel.

Recognition sounds like a straightforward gesture that contains no complications. Typically, it is a mutual gesture between two states of equal legal standing whereby each state recognizes and respects the people, laws, territory and sovereignty of the other. In this case, however, the West, the UN and Israel are seeking a unilateral act by Hamas on behalf of Palestine, i.e., recognizing Israel's right to exist, for which the Palestinian people get nothing in return, because no Israeli obligations are either stated or implied.

In fact, getting Israel to define itself, specify its intentions, and make unequivocal commitments to the peace process, to the Palestinians, or to the Quartet have been the hardest and most enduring blocks to successful peace negotiations. Recognizing Israel, warts and all, therefore, would not be a step forward, either for Hamas or for the Palestinian people.

In short, recognition has to be a product of common understandings reached on what happens next. And those understandings have to be backed with concrete commitments on both sides. Otherwise, the very real prospect is that recognizing Israel, "as is, where is", will be the start of further endless talks that lead nowhere, while the area of a future Palestinian state shrinks and disintegrates under Israeli incursions. Hamas as a political entity will not survive that process, and neither will Palestine.

In response to a request to recognize Israel, even the most forthcoming Hamas team needs a lot of answers:

Which Israel: The one that is now slowly devouring the West Bank and reducing the area of any Palestinian state?

Which Israel: The one that is turning what is left of a Palestinian state into disjointed Bantustans surrounded by a prison wall?

Which Israel: The one that increasingly blocks any Palestinian access to the sacred city of Jerusalem?

Which Israel: The one that has confiscated hundreds of Palestinian farms and villages and confiscates Palestinian lands without compensation?

Which Israel: The one that hogs more and more of Palestine's scarce water?

Which Israel: The one that even now may be planning to assassinate more members of Hamas?

Which Israel: The one that always demands present and real Palestinian concessions for future and undefined Israeli ones?

PALESTINE In Need of a Just God

Which Israel: The one that now occupies the whole of Palestine and day by day makes life miserable for the Palestinian people?

OR: An Israel that unequivocally will pull back to the 1967 truce line to make way for a Palestinian state?

Every one of these Israels, except the last, is simply incompatible with any generally recognized concept of recognition between states. The refusal of Hamas leaders to heed the drumbeat of international opinion would surely be unpopular in the West and in Israel. But at this point Hamas recognition of Israel without any commitments on the part of Israel and/or its international supporters would probably confirm the end of the line for any Palestinian state. Some Israelis and supporters, notably Israeli peace groups such as Gush Shalom, understand this.

It would be only a matter of time before Hamas would turn into the eunuch that Fatah became, or would revert in frustration to insurgency. Hamas knows that recognition without conditions is giving away half of pre-World War II Palestine without a struggle or compensation. That would define the start of future bargaining in the most awkward manner: Basically "as is, where is", recognition says for the Israelis: "What is mine is mine. Now let us talk about how much of yours we're willing to let you keep."

Terrell E Arnold

A less definitive Hamas response appears both possible and constructive: Hamas simply needs to be noncommittal about such issues as the size and shape of Israel; it will refrain from making any statements that appear to take the present situation as a given. Should there be further cracks in the common front of the international community Hamas might simply say it is prepared to accept Israel as the partner to a negotiative process designed to reach a two state solution. And finally, Hamas would make clear that recognition per se would have to await the results of those negotiations.

This is a tough landscape for Hamas because its political personality is not yet fully developed. The present membership of the Hamas leadership group includes not only those who have chosen the active political path, but also varying orders of hardliners who see negotiation as a lost cause and continued armed struggle as a necessity. Membership also includes a number of fairly senior people who have been living outside Palestine, surviving mostly on the good will of surrounding families and governments, and gathering funds, weapons, et cetera to support the cause.

Getting the Hamas political act together could involve a virtual repeat of the Fatah experience. Hamas needs both time and a rationale for getting this disparate membership behind a political agenda. That may require Hamas leadership to ease out some of the hardliners. That task would go more smoothly if outsiders recognized the Hamas position and gave them the needed room. It will go badly for everyone, especially Israel and the Palestinian people, if outsiders and Israel do not recognize and accept this need and cooperate. People simply have to recognize that Hamas won a fair and free election, and the time for serious negotiation of the real issues is now close at hand.

Chapter 6.
Forcibly Renew the Insurgency

2-17-06

Today, less than a month after the insurgent group Hamas decisively won a fair and free election in Palestine, the Israelis, the White House, the State Department, and the US Congress are avidly dedicated to cancelling that victory. But Americans in general are not interested in disenfranchising Hamas. The anti-Hamas gambit is driven by Israeli hardliners in Israel, by Israeli lobbies in Washington, and by avid Israel supporters in the US Government. Why? And what are the probable consequences?

The answer to the first question is Israeli leadership does not want to negotiate. All the fuzzy Israeli play on the so-called Road Map—the peace plan sponsored by the Quartet consisting of the US, Russia, the United Nations, and the European Union—is matched by a not so covert determination to never reach the negotiating table.

Terrell E Arnold

Before he was felled by a stroke, Ariel Sharon was transparent on this matter. He never publicly committed to negotiating the Road Map; he merely avoided actively opposing it. Supporters of the plan simply took his lack of negative comments as a positive state of mind.

Meanwhile, he and the Likud party have proceeded with their own plans: (1) continue building the wall on a course that redefines boundaries, especially around Jerusalem, but elsewhere as well; (2) get free kudos in the west by removing settlements in Gaza because they are difficult and costly to defend, but add settlements that deepen Israeli occupation of the regions around the holy places; (3) harass and make life generally intolerable for Palestinians who live in or near the Jordan Valley; (4) in short, continue elaborating a plan that surrounds and shrinks the spaces that could become a Palestinian state to less than 10% of pre-World War II Palestine. This program is likely to be continued by the new party, Kadima (means "forward" in Hebrew), founded by Sharon before his stroke, and now run by his deputy Ehud Olmert.

The Israeli game plan as espoused by those presently leading the country, does not call for negotiations with the Palestinians, but a Hamas victory, if it cannot be overturned, discredited or ignored, means the Israelis will be faced for the first time with a serious need to negotiate. Moreover, the Palestinian side of the table would be occupied by players who have (a) the support of the people, (b) a reputation for integrity of political action, and (c) carry the stick of possible return to violence if negotiations yield no results.

How to derail Hamas? Enough canny outsiders observed the election so that the results cannot be disputed. It has been argued that the results were not so decisive as a show of support for Hamas, but because Fatah was so inept in running its campaign. That makes little practical difference because Hamas still has a large majority of seats in the assembly. Perhaps, as Hamas opponents have suggested, Mahmoud Abbas and Fatah could be persuaded to keep Hamas out of the cabinet—an undemocratic device—especially in a parliamentary system—for keeping the majority party out of leadership positions. Or, as the outgoing Fatah-dominated parliament decided, a new court could be used to keep Hamas under control. Maybe Abbas could conjure up an excuse to call for early elections. So far no adroit scheme to undo the Hamas victory has been proposed that would be anything but illegal interference with the Palestinian electoral process.

So why not starve the Palestinian people into recognizing they made a mistake? This would be a kind of collective punishment that has been common to Israeli treatment of the Palestinians for more than half a century. What is new is the apparent insistence of the US, the Europeans and the United Nations to deny ongoing assistance to any Hamas government. If Hamas had a track record of mismanaging funds, that might pass muster, but Hamas does not; its reputation for conducting humanitarian programs and managing funds is clean.

Now what? Of course, badger the US Congress into passing a law forbidding assistance to Palestine in the event Hamas comes to power. According to the New York Times, the United States (read the White House and its neo-con supporters) and the Israelis (mainly the Ashkenazim) want to create real hardships for the Palestinian people if Hamas forms a new government at the end of February, as is now expected.

The centerpiece of this effort is H.R. 4681, "The Palestine Anti-Terrorism Act of 2006". That bill, if passed, would cut off all US aid to Palestine if Hamas comes to power. The sole sources of support for this legislation are Israeli supporters in the US Congress, the White House, the State Department, and the Department of Defense who are being hounded by Israeli lobbying groups. This bill now has more than 45 supporters, and you can bet your next paycheck confidently that every one of the sponsors, as well as virtually every other member of the Congress, have actually received Zionist/Israeli campaign contributions and/or have been promised them for the upcoming congressional elections later this year.

The tragedy of this bill is that it is not in the interest of the United States. Nor would the resulting depression and repression of the Palestinian people be in the interest of Israel or Israelis in general. It is surely not in

PALESTINE In Need of a Just God

the interests of the UN membership or the European Community to support it. Why is that so?

HR 4681 is being pushed by the Israeli hardliners to keep any serious negotiation of the Israeli-Palestinian issues from occurring. Without some such action, Israel would be forced to abandon its unilateral actions that now chip away at the future Palestinian state. The hardline and confiscatory takeover of more and more of Palestine so openly sponsored under Sharon and Likud would have to stop. Israel would have to settle for something like the territory mapped by the 1967 green line. While it is reported that the majority of Israelis would settle for this, if it came with real peace, the hardliners want all of Palestine they can get.

To continue its present course, Israel must have the political cover of continuing conflict. HR 4681 is tailor made, because it is more likely to cause terrorism than to stop it. Israel needs the insurgency in order to continue its repressive moves against the Palestinian people. If Hamas reforms and succeeds in controlling other groups such as the al Aqsa Brigades and Palestinian Islamic Jihad, the insurgency is quelled. Israel has no excuse for continuing occupation and repression. Israel then has to face its obligations under peace agreements that Hamas is politically better equipped to negotiate than any previous Palestinian government. The pretense is over.

Terrell E Arnold

If the United States, the United Nations, the European Union, Russia, and Israel collectively frustrate the political will of the Palestinians, they will commit a crime against democracy. The hardships imposed will be a crime against the Palestinian people. The message to the Palestinians is that they are not allowed to choose their own leaders unless the Israelis and the Americans like the choices. This action will hand the gavel to the Hamas hardliners who were brought under significant control to permit Hamas to enter the political process. The hardliners will be convinced, as they indeed already believed, that nothing good can come of negotiations, and that the only answer is persistent armed struggle.

Just what is the US interest in frustrating any Hamas government? If Hamas is suppressed, democracy will be dead in the Middle East as purveyed by the United States. The US, in fact, can expect nothing from this process but trouble: Increasing hostility in the Arab world, new sources of terrorism, less cooperation from regional governments, an increasingly fragile position in the region, weakened relations with all third parties, because no other government profits by the US/Israeli stance. All face enhanced terrorism as a result.

The final tragedy will be the missed opportunity. Long term success in dealing with global terrorism can come only from finding ways to bring many out groups into their societies. The War on Terrorism so far has failed because it does not consider that task important. Insurgents simply must be shown that they can obtain their goals without resorting to violence. The appeal of the Hamas victory is that it represents a breakthrough with an insurgent group. After decades of frustration with all so-called peace processes, the Palestinian people chose their most effective insurgent arm to rule them. Moving successfully on from here will take time and patience at best. But any future home for the Palestinians, and any future peace for the Israelis will depend on making this startling new political gambit work in Palestine.

Chapter 7.
The Diplomacy of Sticks and Stones

2-24-06

Diplomacy is usually a two-sided, mutual exercise of parties of equal standing to achieve mutually agreed outcomes. A new government that comes to power in a country that has been a party to such an exchange is normally expected by the international community—and the other party—to honor such arrangements. So far so good. But what if the new government (say Hamas) is made up of players who have always resisted the allegedly agreed outcomes? And what if that resistance is due to the fact that the other party to such agreements (say any Israeli government so far) has not only failed to live up to the agreements, but has actively violated the understandings at virtually every turn? Just what should be the posture of a new government in these circumstances? Herein lie the subject and the context of today's stiff-arming effort of Israel and supportive foreign objectors against the coming Hamas government in Palestine.

What are the facts? The key documents being waved at Hamas are the Oslo Accords that established

Terrell E Arnold

principles for an interim Palestinian government. Letters of Mutual Recognition were signed under which Israel recognized the PLO as the legitimate representative of the Palestinian people, while the PLO (a) recognized the right of the state of Israel to exist, (b) renounced terrorist violence, and (c) renounced any desire for destruction of Israel.

While the Oslo Accords were progress of sorts, the Israelis recognized the PLO only as representative of the Palestinians; that was not recognition of a Palestinian state. Moreover, all of the final status issues (status of Jerusalem, Israeli settlements in the West Bank and Gaza, the right of Palestinians to return to their homeland, compensation for Israeli-confiscated lands and property, security in Palestine, and borders between Palestine and Israel) were left for later decision. In short, the Accords were long on atmospherics and short on substance.

Three main official addenda to the Oslo Accords were accomplished in meetings at Wye River, Maryland (October 1998), plus sessions at the Sinai resort towns of Sharm el Sheikh (September 1999) and Taba (January 2001). Wye yielded an agreement to pursue final status negotiations with a view to reaching agreement before the end of 1999, but nothing came of that agreement. Talks at Sharm el Sheikh were meant to get the process back on track, essentially to keep things moving. The two sides agreed that neither would initiate nor take any step that would change the status of the West

Bank or Gaza. Readers can judge for themselves how that went. Taba was convened to pursue final status negotiations but ultimately led nowhere, possibly because it occurred too close to an Israeli election for any contending Israeli politician to sign a commitment. In any event, the Israelis started building the infamous wall shortly thereafter, while continuing to add settlement areas in the West Bank and taking harassment actions to reduce the Palestinian population of the Jordan River valley.

A break in the standoff appeared to occur—at the unofficial level—with the Geneva Accords of 2003. If enacted, the Accords would have given Palestine virtually all of the West Bank, the Gaza Strip and part of Jerusalem. They would have adopted the 1967 green line as the device to determine how much territory the Palestinians would receive through a scheme of tradeoffs for certain settlements the Israelis would keep. It would also have limited any right of return—the right of expelled Palestinians to return to their homeland. However, these were accords in name only, because they were not documents attested to by either the PLO or the Israeli government.

While those accords injected a short term burst of hope into the Palestinian situation, that hope was short-lived in Palestine. Rather, Palestinians have seen continued building of the meandering wall, Israeli harassment of Palestinians at countless check points, Israeli construction of Israeli-only roads, continued targeted assassinations of Palestinians, and the steady shrinkage through new settlement activity of any territory for a Palestinian state. The Palestinian counters to these assaults have been sporadic attacks, including suicide bombings.

In the dicey environment of stalled negotiations and steady Israeli incursions on Palestinian territory, the increasingly ill Yasser Arafat and his successor Mahmoud Abbas could offer the Palestinian people little hope. Moreover, neither Arafat nor his successor—assuming that they really wanted to stop them—could totally eliminate insurgent attacks against the Palestine-occupying Israelis.

Palestinians could see that the apparent acceptance of Abbas by the United States and the Israelis had yielded no improvement in their situation and no limitation of the Israeli land grab. Unilateral withdrawal of the Israelis from the Gaza Strip—not a concession to Palestinians, but (as noted earlier) Israeli rejection of an appendage that was costly and difficult to defend—only emphasized the declining control and credibility of Fatah and Mahmoud Abbas. Meanwhile, members of the group Hamas worked diligently at providing the only extensive human services that were available in Palestine. That climate yielded the Hamas election victory.

The truth before the January 25 assembly elections was that outside the realm of third-party rhetoric, a peaceful settlement of the Palestine-Israeli relationship was increasingly unlikely. And none of the Roadmap

PALESTINE In Need of a Just God

managers (the Quartet made up of the US, the UN, the European Union, and Russia) appeared uncomfortable enough with that outlook to do much about it. The situation resembled the fumaroles around a sleeping volcano; no one was moved to do something unless one of the pots bubbled over.

Palestinian patience with this situation has been remarkable. Mainstream Jewish sufferance of it has been equally so. The problem needed a shock. The pot indeed bubbled over. But the most remarkable feature of it is that the pot boiled over at the political not the insurgent level.

United States, European, Israeli and even some Arab reactions to the Hamas victory have been a remarkable study in narrow self-interested squirming. All of them clearly had grown too comfortable with a peace process that was going nowhere and a Palestinian leadership that could do nothing about it. The mere fact that "peace" had become an open-ended "process" said all that could be said about the players' state of mind. In fact, the only bulldozers anywhere near the Middle East peace Roadmap were Israeli ones busily destroying Palestinian homes, villages and orchards, while building a wall to fragment the remainder.

What, sensibly, should Hamas do with this situation? The outraged noises from Israel and outside say "Do what Fatah was doing before the election". That is, stop resisting, recognize Israel's right to exist, and get back to the Roadmap. But Hamas leaders know that any more of the same is a dead end, and so do all serious observers of the situation. The Hamas opportunity lies with unhooking at least temporarily from the past, while seeking to define a new set of rules for the future. Their immediate task is to avoid losing ground while they maneuver to take charge of Palestine's future. That exposes Hamas and the Palestinians to being made miserable by the combination of Israel and the cabal of outsider supporters Israelis have put together to oppose Hamas.

This is an enormous challenge for the outsiders, especially the Quartet. It is essential for them to have in mind and try to keep the key things accomplished at Oslo and in subsequent sessions. But it is vital for the Quartet to face squarely the flaws in this process that can be attributed largely, if not entirely to Israeli hardliner unwillingness to complete a peace agreement. While the view promoted by Israel and its supporters is that they have made numerous concessions, Israel has made none on the status issues, except possibly the land tradeoff unofficially agreed in Geneva but yet to be defined.

As usual, however, the Quartet is focusing entirely on what the Palestinians are supposed to be doing—Quartet definition—versus what Hamas has to do if it is to salvage any real prospect of a Palestinian homeland. The Roadmap simply does not lead there.

PALESTINE In Need of a Just God

The effort of the Israelis is to make the struggle as unequal as possible. Israel now has more or less aligned with it the United States, parts of the European community, and the UN. However, the Russians, the French and a growing number of Arab states are looking for ways to help Hamas and the Palestinians. Most opponents are insisting that Hamas accept as given all that has gone before. But that trail is littered with accumulating Palestinian concessions for which there have been no real—that is here now or final status—Israeli ones. The language is one-sided and pre-emptive. Israel wants its right to exist to be recognized, but it has yet to recognize Palestine as an entity. Israel wants the Palestinians to accept all of the "accomplishments" and the "framework" of the Oslo accords and subsequent talks, but accepting all of that only circumscribes anything the Palestinians may ask for. Meanwhile, as facts on the ground demonstrate, the Palestinians have lost ground at each stage.

The Israeli tactics are neat. Without ever promising anything, in the past three weeks they have aligned the governments of over half a billion people on the side of making the Palestinians concede major diplomatic points to Israel for which there is no quid pro quo offered or suggested. The Israelis have used the United States and a few others in that manner for half a century, never presenting themselves as the principal party to a negotiation in which they had to be prepared to make concessions in exchange for concessions and live with outcomes in exchange for like responses from the other party.

People may argue with that judgment, but the real issues—the final status questions of right of return, compensation for confiscated lands and property, access to Jerusalem, territorial definitions and boundary determinations—always have been reserved to the future. Palestinian negotiators regularly have lost in these uneven matches, because no concessions have been made by Israel on the key issues.

Israel's present gambit is to keep its support structure well-oiled and never present itself for negotiation, merely wait for Hamas to collapse under the extreme pressure of the Israeli support group. Then things can get comfortably back to the "peace process" which, as of now, is not designed to go anywhere. The key issues of interest to the Palestinians are not on the table, and the Israelis keep accumulating facts on the ground to distort the eventual outcome more in their favor. Immediate Israeli targets are all lands of the Jordan River Valley.

Israel knows, however, that their neat situation won't endure if Palestinian negotiators are given any room to maneuver. The first gambits sound reasonable: Honor the Oslo accords, recognize Israel's right to exist, and give up terrorism. However, Fatah and Palestinian Authority accession to those rules have virtually enabled the disassembly of any future Palestinian state. Palestinians have been giving ground regularly, if not steadily, since World War II, and many of them have been on the run since the massacre of Deir Yassin village in 1948 and subsequent destruction of more than 400 other Palestinian communities. That process continues in the West Bank while Israel's supporters look on silently or pursue the so-called "quiet diplomacy" that never openly confronts Israeli excesses, and has led to the present debacle.

The present tactic is to beat the Palestinians into retreat from their electoral decision. It is the diplomacy of sticks and stones: Stop passing revenues to the Palestinian Authority that legally belong to them—even though collected as an agreed procedure by the Israelis. Retrieve $50 million in US assistance that was promised by Bush to Abbas during the latter's "state" visit. Withhold other US funds. Re-examine UN funding of support and infrastructure programs. In short, starve enough Palestinians, and make life miserable for them so that they, in turn, will withdraw their support for Hamas, or prevent that support from evolving into the kind of national unity government that Hamas seems to prefer. All of this is being undertaken without any real public pressure in the US, the UN or Western Europe except from Israeli lobbies.

The net effect of these gambits is to (a) assume the worst about Hamas performance, and then (b) do everything possible to make that outcome inevitable.

Terrell E Arnold

Some of the side effects are pretty horrendous: (1) the Palestine problem is actively being recast as a struggle between the West and Islam; (2) countries whose support for terrorism has consisted largely of aid to the Palestinian insurgencies—Syria and Iran most obviously—will enhance their support; (3) increased support by any Islamic country for Hamas will be viewed by the US and Israel particularly as further promotion of Islamic terrorism, no matter what a Hamas government does with the support; (4) active terrorist groups in Islam and the rest of the world as well will respond in variously sympathetic ways to the repression of the Palestinians by a collective "West"; (5) the US-led War on Terrorism will receive a wholly gratuitous boost from this attempt to nullify a free and fair Palestinian election; and (6) the US-promoted democratization effort will be confirmed by its critics as the misbegotten propaganda gimmick they already thought it was.

There are a comparative few compelling voices on the side of a more honorable and likely to be constructive approach. One is former President Jimmy Carter; another is an American attorney, John Whitbeck, who has provided legal advice to the Palestinians for a number of years. In the past few days, Egypt's President Mubarak has said no to a US request to deny assistance to Palestine. Iran has publicly promised assistance in a meeting between Iranian President Ahmadinijad and Khaled Mesha'al, the exiled Hamas leader in Damascus.

PALESTINE In Need of a Just God

In a Washington Post op-ed of February 20, President Carter observes that the election of Hamas cannot harm "genuine peace talks", since such talks "have been nonexistent for more than five years". He also notes that on behalf of the PLO Mahmoud Abbas has sought peace talks for the past year (he does not note that there was no Israeli response). President Carter basically concludes that the Palestinians should not be punished for their electoral decision and Hamas should be given room to transit from insurgency to a position of political authority.

Whitbeck steps right into the middle of the negotiative process, a space he has occupied periodically for nearly two decades. His suggestion, as published widely in the Arab press, is that Hamas should take the initiative now and "publicly announce its support for the Arab League's Beirut Declaration of March 2002". In that declaration, all Arab states (including Palestine) offered Israel permanent peace and normal diplomatic and economic relations in return for Israel's returning to pre-1967 borders. Note that by this declaration Palestine accepted the existence of Israel and if Hamas issued a statement of public support for that declaration, it would be de facto accepting the existence of Israel, without necessarily saying so.

Whitbeck's next point is pretty pithy. Under Hamas, he says Palestinian leadership "should make clear that, after 39 years of foreign military occupation, the Palestinian people can no longer tolerate the cynical series of never-ending peace plans (including the current Roadmap) designed by others simply to postpone the necessary and obvious choices and to string out forever a perpetual "peace process" while further entrenching the occupation with new "facts on the ground".

As Whitbeck summarizes the situation, over the years the Israelis have been offered many carrots, and they have not reacted favorably to any of them, and they should now be shown a stick. To this end, "the new Palestinian leadership should simultaneously declare (preferably with the concurrence of President Mahmoud Abbas and Fatah) that, if Israel does not publicly agree to proceed toward a two-state solution in accordance with the Beirut Declaration by a reasonable date (say, three months hence), the Palestinian people will consider that Israel has definitively rejected a two-state solution in favor of a one-state solution and, accordingly, will thereafter seek their liberation and self-determination through citizenship in a single democratic state in all of pre-1948 Palestine, free of all forms of discrimination and with equal rights for all who live there."

The choice, states Whitbeck, should be for the Israelis to choose between a two-state solution based on the Arab League's Beirut Declaration of 2002, or "a one-state solution in accordance with fundamental democratic principles". He says the key would be "to let the Israeli people choose whichever of those two alternatives Israelis prefer and to accept Israel's choice." However, he is well aware that many Palestinians prefer the one-state solution, because it preserves for them the rights of citizenship in their native Palestine, would eliminate refugee status for several million Palestinians, and would recognize their status as people of equal worth with the Israelis.

If such a proposal were to lead to an Israeli response that shows genuine will to negotiate and resolve the long-standing issues, Hamas would have tools to restrain, and eventually tame the Palestinian hardliners, not only those in Hamas, but in other groups such as the al Aqsa Brigades and Palestinian Islamic Jihad. The vehicle for that, some indicate, would be an old trick of Mohammad the Prophet, to declare a truce of indeterminate length—even unto a generation—that would create and sustain the climate for constructive talks.

If that approach yields no results, it will be reprehensible for the Israeli support group to insist that the Palestinians come to heel, while the Israelis do nothing to deserve their consideration. It is time for the "West" to adopt a posture toward this situation that makes sense in terms of its realities. The Palestinians will not endure continuing repression and confiscation of their remaining homeland without fighting back. The cure for terrorism in this case is insistence on fairness and actual movement toward conditions for a decent life for both Palestinians and Israelis. The Israeli promoted effort to suppress Hamas, if it were to succeed, would guarantee a future of terrorism and warfare for both.

Chapter 8.
'It's Really That Simple'

3-8-06

There is no process more important to the future welfare of societies in revolt than the transition from insurgency to civil governance. That being said, there is no historic example where the process has been short, simple, without contention, and successful, all in a tidy sequence. Sometimes, as in the French Revolution, the insurgents end up being successful, but they fall into conflict about how to proceed, and the interregnum can be long, unstable and bloody. That is partly because revolutionaries tend to be poor governors. In the French case, even so, the end product—several years later—was a republic. The lesson of history on this is that moving on from rebellion is at best dicey and complicated. As demonstrated too often in the French case, a corollary lesson is that outside interference generally makes matters worse, especially for the society in revolt.

No two cases appear exactly alike, because no two human situations ever quite mirror image each other. In some respects, the pattern resembles the way someone has said penguins feed the seals: They stand around on the ice, jostling each other, until somebody falls off. That often works. However, in a century increasingly saturated with people who are, in turn, increasingly saturated with weapons, relying on the outcome of an accident appears inordinately high risk.

A more deliberate procedure is urgently called for. The United States has advertised for decades that the "more deliberate procedure", one that is widely approved throughout the world, is regime change by democratic election. Speaking strictly of what the people in the affected country or group may want, that procedure is frequently reliable. The hangup is that protracted insurgencies tend to delay any trip to the voting booth, either because the powers that be are reluctant to hold an election because they might lose, or the insurgents are reluctant to get involved in an election because they do not trust the outcome, or interested outsiders do not think the timing or players or agenda are right, or all three. This system actually works best when all significant contending parties are committed to the process and the outcome. It is most likely to fail when any of the major contenders or significant outside interests try to jigger either the rules or the results.

Palestine's date with this process was long in coming. For more than three quarters of a century, beginning immediately after World War I, the Palestinian people have been subjected to assault, confiscation of their homes and properties, and expulsion from their

PALESTINE In Need of a Just God

native land. Only in the late 1960s did Palestinian advocates begin to spell out the rights of the Palestinian people and seek voices for them in their future, especially respecting how and where they lived. But from the beginning, the usurper of those rights and interests had one or more big brother protectors who regularly shielded it from the consequences of excess, including mounting crimes against humanity.

With no external political sponsor or direct defender of their rights, the Palestinians began to fight back. Their first major vehicle was the Palestine Liberation Organization (PLO), founded by Yasser Arafat and led also by the current President Mahmoud Abbas (PLO name: Abu Mazen). The PLO was closely paced by formation of the Popular Front for the Liberation of Palestine—a very active terrorist group in its early years that eventually merged with the PLO and stopped exporting terrorism. Beginning with the earliest Camp David meetings during the Carter Administration, the PLO moved toward a governing body of the Palestinian people and largely foreswore terrorism.

Even so, the Palestinian people continued to lose ground. More lands were confiscated, villages were eradicated. The refugee population of the West Bank and Gaza grew, while surrounding countries and the outside world became home to thousands of Palestinian refugees.

Reacting to this continuing pattern of abuse and repression, Hamas was created by its founder, Sheikh

Terrell E Arnold

Ahmad Yassin in 1987. Hamas is said to be an offshoot of the Muslim Brotherhood, an Islamic fundamentalist group active in Egypt and other Arab countries. It is also said to have been adopted and used by the Israelis as a foil to Fatah and the PLO. That may have been so, but Yassin was assassinated by the Israelis in 2004. His successor was assassinated by the Israelis shortly thereafter.

Hamas means "zeal" or "enthusiasm" in Arabic, but it is also an acronym for Islamic Resistance Movement. Under Yassin the group established itself fairly quickly as an insurgency, but even more so as a provider of human services to many truly downtrodden people in the refugee camps. Most of the Hamas budget, estimated at $70 million yearly, has gone for human services.

Since 1993, Hamas is said to have carried out more than 350 attacks causing more than 500 deaths. That means however, that Hamas has conducted small harassment attacks—mortars, short range rockets, small arms, and suicide bombings—involving usually few casualties per attack, and sometimes none.

That compares with Israel Defense Force operations in the same period that caused thousands of Palestinian casualties and destroyed much of the Palestinian infrastructure, including the entire town of Jenin. A particularly bad example was destruction of an entire apartment building in an effort to eliminate one militant.

A defacto force in local politics from its beginning, because of its human services activities, Hamas entered the political arena slowly, capturing a number of municipal seats in 2004, but it boycotted the presidential election of 2005 that brought Mahmoud Abbas to power. Deciding to enter the 2006 People's Assembly elections in January 2006, Hamas was predicted to have a good showing, but its win of a solid majority of seats was a surprise.

As largely uncontested head of the PLO and later the Palestinian Authority, Yasser Arafat and his successor Mahmoud Abbas have been looked to by outsiders, notably the Israelis and the United States, but also the UN and European governments, to moderate the behavior of all Palestinians and to shut down the insurgent organizations.

The Israelis tried to shut them down by arrests and assassinations—killing at least five leaders of Hamas and subjecting such leading insurgent figures as Marwan Barghouti, the founder of the al Aqsa Brigades, to long prison sentences. Arafat brought the PFLP into alliance with the PLO, and over time PFLP terrorist operations ceased outside the land area of Palestine and Israel.

Threats, cajolery, arrests and torture did not serve to shut down Palestinian insurgent activities, because

Terrell E Arnold

the Israelis never stopped their programs of confiscation, expulsion, and harassment—efforts that in other hands have been labeled ethnic cleansing. . Far from being reduced, the land grab and the repressive treatment of Palestinians have grown in the past five years. Even so, under mounting pressure from the Palestinian Authority, Fatah (the PLO translated into a political party) and outsiders of the Quartet charged with pursuing the Roadmap peace negotiations (the US, UN, European Union, and Russia), Hamas declared a truce more than a year ago as part of its preparation to enter the political process. This truce was the first significant step since reform of the PLO toward transition of a Palestinian insurgent group toward political participation. This truce is still in place.

It is remarkable that the truce has held despite continuing Israeli targeted assassinations of Palestinian "militants", continued imprisonment and torture of Hamas, al Aqsa Brigade, PIJ and other Palestinian insurgents, and harassment of Palestinians throughout the West Bank, Gaza, and increasingly in and around the Jordan River Valley.

Meanwhile, it is clear that Hamas has grown in real political terms due to the needs of its members and their families, as well as other Palestinians. Not only did it have an insurgency related network, it had a well-developed social services and welfare network. In effect, Hamas had already transited a great distance toward non-insurgent and political participation in Palestinian life. Preparation for and participation in the January 2006 assembly elections were its first concrete public steps toward taking a leading role in governance.

In public statements in the past few weeks, notably an interview with a Washington Post reporter, the new Hamas chosen Prime Minister, Ismail Haniyeh made it clear that Hamas is thinking in terms of some combination of the Geneva Accords and the Arab League's Beirut Declaration of March 2002 as a framework for future negotiations. Those two together would provide for a two state system following the 1967 truce lines between Israel and Palestine save for some possible trades of territory in the north for settlements around Jerusalem. That proposal, as reported, essentially avoided recognition of Israel until the Israelis declared themselves on the terms of a final settlement.

It is obvious to close observers of the situation that the Israeli hardliners do not want to face that solution. If Hamas sticks to its guns, and is able to bring the majority of the Palestinians along, the only way out of the situation would be to negotiate. With an Israeli election a mere three weeks away, no such Israeli commitment is likely to be forthcoming. The preferred Israeli hardliner remedy in the meantime is to arrange an accident, something that will discredit Hamas, and cause the Palestinians to cluster around Fatah and the present leadership of Mahmoud Abbas, with whom the process can be bent back toward protracted negotiations under

Terrell E Arnold

the so-called Roadmap that are intended by the Israeli hardliners to go nowhere.

Given the Israeli history of hardliner behavior in such circumstances, an "accident" could be anything from a false flag terrorist event blamed on Hamas, to further assassinations of Hamas leaders (Israeli hardliners have now declared intent to do so), or to a contrived rejection of Hamas by the Palestinian people. That could be most readily undertaken by trying to starve the Palestinians, while getting that blamed on Hamas. Israeli resort to usual dirty tricks could arouse predictable international outrage, but starving the Palestinians into line appears to have some resonance, especially with US leadership, the UN and some European governments.

This choice is remarkably but not unpredictably dim witted. Getting it done has every Israeli lobby in every capital of importance working overtime. Trying to bring Arab governments into line on her trip through the Middle East last week, Secretary of State Condoleezza Rice tried unsuccessfully to get them to go along. Her view, expressed enroute, was the US will not do business with Hamas because it is a terrorist group. "It's really that simple" she said. The fact that the US in the past has done a great deal of business with terrorist groups such as the Israeli Stern and Irgun group founders and leaders, the Contras in Nicaragua, or the UNITAS group in Angola (whose leader Jonas Savimbi met with White House officials per arrangements by Oliver North in the mid-1980s), all in a Republican administration at that, appears to have escaped her.

Perhaps the key would be to get the Congress to starve the Palestinians. Before the House of Representatives at the moment is House Bill 4681 which, if passed, would deny any US assistance to a Hamas led government in Palestine. That bill, thanks to the forceful arm-twisting and lobbying by Israeli supporters, has nearly 90 sponsors, having slowly added new ones over the past few weeks who are looking anxiously to their upcoming contests in November and hope to pocket the Jewish vote in advance. While the bill is not in the US interest, has no supporters other than Israeli interest groups, and would further alienate Islamic societies if enacted, it may well come to pass.

Yet another solution would be to expel all Palestinians from the West Bank, Gaza and, of course, Israel itself, to the east bank of the Jordan River. That means literally to take the remaining properties, lands and orchards of the Palestinians without compensation, and force the people to move to the Hashemite Kingdom of Jordan. As a number of hardline Zionists, including Ariel Sharon, have put it, Jordan would be Palestine. Already a significant share of the population of Jordan is Palestinian, many of whom have lived in that region for generations, but many refugees are from Israel or Palestine west of the Jordan. With the enormous investment of time and money that Israeli supporters have made in capturing the American political system, as well as

Terrell E Arnold

significant parts of European systems, the hope is that Israel could do this without rebellion from those countries.

There is an ironic historical twist in the pressure on Hamas to recognize Israel's right to exist. It is well worth reciting here the founding document, the Declaration of November 1917 by Lord Balfour of Great Britain that simply reads: "His Majesty's Government view with favor the establishment in Palestine of a National Home for the Jewish people, and will use their best endeavors to facilitate the achievement of this object, *it being clearly understood that nothing shall be done which may prejudice the civil and religious rights of existing non-Jewish communities in Palestine, (italics added)* or the rights and political status enjoyed by Jews in any other country." Providing land in Palestine for a Palestinian state (about equal to land for Israel) was a central part of the 1947 UN partition plan. By expelling Palestinians from their homes and repressing those who stay in Palestine, Israel is violating the terms of its foundation, in effect violating its right to exist. The very terms of its existence become thereby a proper subject for negotiation.

All gambits to avoid facing the Palestinians fairly and squarely require that the Hamas victory in Palestine somehow be frustrated. The deepest Israeli hardliner fear, barely buried under present argument and squirming, is that, if allowed to prosper, Hamas will stick to its guns, force final settlement negotiations on terms that are actually consistent with the overall thrust of Oslo,

Geneva and related peace initiatives, as well as the intent of the Balfour Declaration and UN decisions, and effectively put an end to the conflict. If Hamas proposes negotiations along the lines of the Geneva Accords and the Arab League proposal mentioned earlier, everybody but the Israeli hardliners are likely to be prepared to go along. That would indeed be awkward.

The immediate victims of any of the Israeli gambits to frustrate Hamas will be the Palestinian people, but a particularly disturbing victim would be the effort of Hamas to become a political force and renounce violence. How serious it is about this transition can only be tested by giving Hamas room. If given room, Hamas political leadership, which now has considerable sway over the movement, could prevail and the truce now in effect would hold for the indefinite future while negotiations progress. If Fatah and the PLO are encouraged by the US and Israel or others to undercut or bypass Hamas and go back to a negotiative process that predictably will lead nowhere, then Hamas political leadership will lose ground. Along with other terrorist groups, who have been fairly quiet for some time, the insurgent arm of Hamas will be revived. The flow of resources from Arab and Palestinian donors around the world will continue.

A few organizations are actively working to avert this catastrophe, and a large number of Jews in the United States, European countries and in Israel oppose what Israeli hardliners are doing to the Palestinians. In Washington, the Council for the National Interest

Terrell E Arnold

Foundation, a group of retired diplomats and other former officials, is seeking to avert passage of HR 4681 while working to avoid cuts in assistance to Palestine. In Israel, the peace group Gush Shalom is trying to muster Israeli public opinion around a solution that favors at least a wait and see Israeli posture. Offering some hope, it appears that European governments and the UN are reviewing their earlier gut reactions to the Hamas victory. Washington official reactions are actually more mixed than the knee-jerk White House early reactions indicated. Arab governments are simply not signing on to efforts to undercut Hamas, even though they may have their own worries about the Muslim Brotherhood in their countries. Hamas itself is proceeding cautiously, avoiding provocation, while not giving away anything important to future negotiations.

In Moscow, Putin is said to be exerting heavy pressure on Hamas visitors to recognize Israel's right to exist. So far the Hamas visitors have held their ground, because as they and many outside observers see it, to go back to business as usual means the end of Palestine.

If efforts to give Hamas some room fail, the Israeli hardliners and dreamers of a greater Israel will have their way. Continuing conflict will permit them to do what they have been doing for virtually half a century: (1) relying on the US to defend their right to "defend themselves" while (2) arming themselves to the teeth largely at US expense, (3) by force and intimidation taking the whole of Palestine away from the Palestin-

PALESTINE In Need of a Just God

ian people, (4) increasing the pressures of poverty and repression to get Palestinians to leave, and (5) avoiding any compensation to the four million people or more who will be dispossessed. Palestine will become a "free country" for the Israelis who occupy it. To apply what Secretary Rice said in trying to undercut Hamas: "It's really that simple."

Chapter 9.
HR 4681: For Terrorism - Against the Palestinian People

3-28-6

The House of Representatives is about to begin markup on House Resolution 4681, the so-called Palestinian Anti-Terrorism Act of 2006. This resolution would prohibit the United States from providing direct assistance to the Palestine Authority unless the President certifies that the Authority has met the subjective and ambiguous conditions outlined below. Markup is the usual step that precedes sending a bill to the floor for a vote. One can ask why this bill is bound for the House floor, when it has no known organized support from the American public, addresses no issue of impact on the welfare of Americans, and flies in the face of the considered views of many American allies.

Terrell E Arnold

This bill is moving because it has almost 200 sponsoring members of Congress who have been cozened, promised campaign contributions or intimidated into supporting it by the American Israel Public Affairs Committee and other Israel support groups. AIPAC's immediate leverage is that all members of the House are up for reelection in November. For any Member of Congress, the assurance of votes or of campaign funds will be critical in the next few months. An about equal incentive, however, is the fact that AIPAC has funded the defeat of several members of Congress who in the past refused to cooperate and support Israeli interests.

HR 4681 is one of the most mischievous pieces of legislation to appear in the Congress in years. That becomes obvious as its eight stated objectives are examined.

This bill starts by declaring that "It shall be the policy of the United States to support emergence of a democratic Palestinian governing authority that"

1. "Denounces and combats terrorism." The target of this legislation, Hamas, declared and has maintained a truce for more than a year, campaigned successfully in a free and fair election and won a majority in the Palestinian People's Assembly. Isn't that at least a significant step in the desired direction?

2. "Has agreed to and is taking action to disarm and dismantle any terrorist agency, network, or facility".

Hamas is supposed to have the authority and will to do those things while under a publicly announced Israeli threat to assassinate its leaders, including the newly designated Prime Minister of Palestine.

3. "Has agreed to work to eliminate anti-Israel and anti-Semitic incitement and the commemoration of terrorists in Palestinian society". And this must be done while Israel continues to confiscate lands, hog water, create roads that are for Israelis only and divide Palestine into fragments where Palestinians are forced by Israeli occupation to live in sub-human conditions. It would be a supreme act of will not to be anti-Israel in these circumstances. Since the Palestinians are Semites, while the Ashkenazim Zionists who persecute them are not, anti-Semitism is actually being practiced on the Palestinians.

4. "Has agreed to respect the boundaries and sovereignty of its neighbors." The only boundary between Israel and Palestine that has international standing, the 1967 Green Line, is constantly violated by Israelis who continue to take additional lands for settlements, while harassing Palestinians to leave the areas of Jerusalem and the Jordan Valley. The likely winners of Israel's March 28 elections have touted their intent to act unilaterally and take all of Palestine.

5. "Acknowledges, respects, the human rights of all peoples." The human rights shoe is on the other foot. The Palestinians are expected to accept willingly the

Terrell E Arnold

status of second class citizenship in Israel for those who live there, and to live under the sub-human conditions imposed by Israeli occupation. By any objective standard, Israel is guilty of continuing war crimes against the Palestinian people.

6. "Conducts free, fair, and transparent elections in compliance with international standards." In January the Palestinians actually did that, but HR 4681 is designed to undercut a democratically elected Palestinian National Authority. The bill declares that because the Palestinians elected leadership that the neighbors or the American Congress do not like, the Palestinian people shall be punished.

7. "Ensures institutional and financial transparency and accountability." The leadership that has a proven track record for doing this happens to be Hamas, but HR 4681 gives no credit.

8. "Has agreed to recognize the State of Israel as an independent, sovereign, Jewish, democratic state." The Palestinians can do nothing to assure Israeli independence, sovereignty, Jewishness, or democracy; they can only agree to Israel's right to exist, but in a world of even minimal fairness, Israel would have to give the Palestinians equal recognition.

In short, the entire purpose of HR 4681 is to impose by American legislative fiat a Middle East peace settlement that serves Israeli interests while giving the Palestinians nothing. If the Palestinians comply with this act, they get only a small order of freedom from American harassment. They will remain under the sub-human conditions of continuing Israeli occupation and face continuing theft of their lands, no matter what they do.

The most striking feature of this bill is not the electoral support members of Congress undoubtedly have been promised to pass it. The truly nasty feature of the bill is the obvious fact that it was drafted by AIPAC-the agent of a foreign government, and use of the US Congress by Israeli lobbies to keep Israeli leadership from having to negotiate fairly with the Palestinian people. It is clear to serious Palestine watchers that, if given the chance, Hamas has some ability to push the Israeli-Palestine relationship toward genuine negotiations for the first time ever. Meanwhile, the Israeli elections, whoever wins, are unlikely to yield new Israeli leadership that is willing to negotiate. The more likely outcome is an Israeli leadership that is dedicated to unilateral actions meant to assure eventual Israeli possession of all of Palestine.

Those prospects contain no recipe for Palestinian reform or prosperity. If this bill is passed, and the Palestinian people are subjected to hardships that cause them to reject Hamas—the clear purpose of this act— then the Palestinian/Israeli conflict will continue and eventually grow worse. Frustration will drive more Palestinians into terrorism. Sympathy for them will drive others into support for terrorism or active involvement in terrorist attacks. The international terrorism generator that Palestine has been for decades will be reignited full blast. Under cover of that conflict, Israel will continue to confiscate Palestinian lands until it reaches the Jordan and the Palestinian people are all expelled.

Shame on the US Congress for being a willing party to such a plan.

Chapter 10. Palestinian Repression - The Intended Consequences

6-18-06

Following the January 2006 election of Hamas as the ruling party in Palestine, the United States, Israel, the European Union and the UN conspired to withhold assistance to any Hamas-led government in order to bring it down. The agreed procedure, clear and callus in its brutality, was to teach the Palestinians a lesson in modern western concepts of democracy: Having a fair and open election was great, but selecting a leadership the Western cabal did not like was a costly mistake, and the Palestinian people collectively would be punished for their bad judgment. From that point onward the financial screws on Palestine have been tightened, and on Monday, June 12, the International Committee of the Red Cross said the situation could turn into a "major humanitarian emergency."

Terrell E Arnold

The ICRC judgment, predictable from the first day of the collective Western decision to deny Palestinian aid, is unlikely to have any effect on the perpetrators of this humanitarian crime. The intent, loosely put, is to bring down any Hamas government, however constructive it might be, and bring the Palestinians back to a negotiating frame of mind with Israel. That means they must buy into a Fatah, Mahmoud Abbas led process of agreeing to everything the Israelis want, while the Israelis will continue to agree to nothing the Palestinians want or need. Here, once more, the Israelis have enlisted the West to do the dirty work for the Zionists, while Israel's new leadership under Ehud Olmert prepares openly to add more settlements, to complete walling in the Palestinians and to add the Jordan Valley to Israel.

This all began when Hamas broke the house rule on negotiations with Israel: They proposed preconditions to recognizing Israel that required actual Israeli concessions. But under Israeli rules—tacitly accepted by the West—the Palestinians simply cannot ask for anything in return for concessions; they can only agree with Israeli dictates. Shortly after it won the January 2006 election, Hamas indicated it would accept a two state solution based on a return to the 1967 green line, a capital in Jerusalem and recognition of other Palestinian rights. That is a basic position previously agreed upon by the Arab League. A recent survey of key Palestinian political prisoners in Israeli prisons showed they also accept that basic position.

PALESTINE In Need of a Just God

By denying aid to the Hamas-led government, the Israeli goal is to get back to safe but pointless negotiating territory with Fatah and Mahmoud Abbas in charge. That, the Israeli Zionist leadership thinks, will quash, once and for all, any prospect of a Palestinian state. That cannot be done with Hamas in power, so Hamas has to go.

But where will Hamas go? With the known history of Middle East violence, that question urgently needs consideration. The West and Israel seem hell-bent on skewering themselves, and, as the well-known maxim holds, ignoring history and living to repeat it.

Ever since Yasser Arafat began to mobilize the Palestinians around the idea of a national home, Middle East violence has been on the rise. This pattern of violence has been fired by the fact that the Israelis ruthlessly have emptied hundreds of Palestinian villages of their people, and forced those people into refugee camps or exile. Palestinian insurgency and, by export, international terrorism had their main roots in this problem. There were few international terrorist incidents of any kind before the Israelis began wholesale dispossession of the Palestinian people. No Middle East terrorist group of international consequence existed before wholesale expulsion of the Palestinians began.

Only when there was some hope among Palestinians that their situation might improve through negotiation did the growth of terrorism of Middle East origin begin to level off. It has waxed and waned in loose fashion with the promise, or lack of promise of the peace process as perceived by the Palestinian people or their supporters. Before the Iraq War, at least half of the known Middle East militant groups were outgrowths of the Palestinian problem. The others were local groups aimed at bringing change or bringing down their local governments in places such as Egypt, Saudi Arabia, and others. In short, virtually all Middle East terrorist groups Westerners know anything about sprang from Israeli repression of the Palestinians.

That Palestinian repression is the mother of most Middle East terrorism has been obvious to anyone who cared to examine the situation. However, the point seems lost on the loose Western cabal now bent on bringing about the political downfall of Hamas. But here are some critical facts. Sabri al Banna, whose war name was Abu Nidal, the earlier of two "heroic" terrorist enemies of the West, grew out of the Palestine problem. Credited, or better, charged with over 900 attacks, he was eased into semi-retirement partly by the peace process, partly by US and other efforts to contain him, until he died in 2002 in Baghdad. However, his disagreement with Arafat over the utility of negotiations with Israel has been proven more right than wrong over the years.

The second "heroic" terrorist enemy of the West has been Abu Musab al Zarqawi, who was a Jordan-born Palestinian. Hardly known before the overthrow of Saddam Hussein, al Zarqawi's work has been in the context of the Iraqi resistance against the US/Coalition occupation of Iraq. While the Iraq War has become its own breeding ground for terrorists, the odds are that any "terrorist" with enough experience and recognition to succeed al Zarqawi will have been brought up on the Palestine resistance experience.

Three Middle East countries have borne the brunt of Western irritation with Middle East terrorism. Syria, Iraq, and Iran, all charter members of the US State Department log of terrorism sponsoring states, are on the list principally, if not entirely, for their support of Palestinian groups. In effect, they are labeled "terrorism sponsoring states" because they have abetted the Palestinian insurgency against Israeli occupation and repression of the Palestinian people. The United States could support the Contras in Nicaragua or Jonas Savimbi's UNITA in Angola (both insurgent/terrorist groups in the 1980s) without labeling itself a terrorism sponsoring state, while at that same time pinning the label on the three Middle East countries.

Given that history, the chances are that Zarqawi's reported successor, Sheikh Abu Hamza al Muhajir, will have a history in one or both of the world's major terrorism generators—the Palestinian struggle or the US supported Mujahidin fight against Russia in Afghanistan. A US military spokesman in Iraq has suggested that Abu Hamza al Muhajir may be a pseudonym for Abu Ayyub al Masri, an Egyptian, but the dominant theme in his description is that he is an "experienced jihadist". If he is Abu Ayyub, his experience appears to have been gained alongside Osama bin Laden in the Afghanistan war with Russia. If true, ironically he, as well as Osama, is a product of American training in Afghanistan. It can pretty much be taken as given that he shares Osama's support for the Palestinians, or more accurately the hate born of Israeli repression of the Palestinians.

The clear message for US, European, Israeli and UN leadership is that the principal training ground for Middle East terrorists has been the Palestine insurgency. That being so, the West collectively, and the Israelis specifically are taking a horrendous chance by causing Hamas to fail. If Hamas fails, the likely prospect is that everybody in the West will pay for it with a resurgence of terrorist violence, first in Israel and more widely spread among Western targets. Failure to give the Hamas political wing the time needed to bring the hardliners along on a political process will simply undercut any Hamas effort to transform the movement into a political party.

For more than half a century the Israelis have slowly stolen Palestine from its people, and they have done that with more or less constant US aid and support. The effort to suppress Hamas turns that pattern into a collective Western assault on Palestine. As the Palestinians suffer, their treatment by the West will be seen by Muslims as a generalized assault on Islam, a repeat of the Crusades. Added to numerous reported abuses by US forces in Iraq, legend will center not merely on treatment of the men, but on the brutal starving, killing and abuse of women and children.

Many Israelis do not agree with the agenda being pursued by Ehud Olmert's ruling coalition. Based on reports from Israeli peace activists such as Uri Avnery, the odds are that a majority would settle for a two state solution bounded by the 1967 Green Line, if that brought enduring peace. A significant number disapprove of the occupation and repression of the Palestinian people. How is it then, one might ask, that the occupation, the land grab, the creeping Israeli expansion go on, if so many people oppose them?

Politics in the United States is now a model for the answer. The US is following policies that are driven by a small cabal of single-minded military expansionists who are supported by a Congress whose members grow fat on the contributions of the military, industrial and financial lobbies who profit from military expansion. America's reputation, economic security, the lives of young men and women killed and maimed in a pointless war, all are sacrifices to the profits of that Washington cabal. What the people may want, as the cabal sees it, is unimportant.

Israeli politics operate much the same way, no matter how democratic the process may look. The Ashkenazi Zionist cabal that makes Israeli decisions on war and peace has never been out of power. In their hands, with no regard for Palestinian rights, the slow absorption of all of Palestine goes on, regardless of what many Israeli citizens may want.

Some powerful individuals, such as former Mossad chief Ephraim Halevy, have said publicly that causing Hamas to fail is a mistake. Under a Zionist leadership that brutally suppresses dissent, there are simply not enough opposing voices.

The world was sufficiently divided when only the US was paired with Israel in repressing the Palestinians. A virtually total Western alliance aimed at starving the Palestinians to suppress Hamas, or to bypass Hamas and force its failure, will strengthen the Islamic extremist charge of a Western war on Islam.

According to some observers, a very active version of the Western strategy is to provoke a civil war in Palestine. There are enough deep-seated differences between Fatah and Hamas to bring that about, and Hamas has sufficient reason to believe Fatah, at least Mahmoud Abbas, is supporting the assault being launched on the Hamas government, mainly by the US and Israel. The Europeans, perhaps without enthusiasm, are supporting this effort.

The tragedy of the likely outcome is that the West must take credit for the renewal of terror in and around the Middle East. As a result of the boycott of assistance to Palestine, Hamas has already ended its unilateral truce. The superficial intended consequence may be a

PALESTINE In Need of a Just God

US-Israeli effort to jolt the Palestinian people back into a placid compliance with Israeli wishes. The actual intended consequence for the Zionists is to restore the enemy they need to cover their continuing takeover of what is left of Palestine.

The Palestinians, as always, will be the losers, because they will have made no progress toward a settlement with the Israelis, and, with the failure of Hamas, they will have lost their only promising political sponsor. Fortunately for humanity only a few of the repressed Palestinians become militants and insurgents. In the West, in the United States particularly, those few who fight back against Israeli repression will be blamed for all the violence in Palestine. But the next generation of "heroic" enemies of the West and Israel will grow in that newly re-fertilized soil.

The next "heroic" enemy of the West may not be a Palestinian, but, if not, he (or she) is very likely to be someone who thinks, quite sanely, that the Palestinian people are being brutally repressed, and that the perpetrators should be made to pay for it. In either case, the Bush administration War on Terrorism will be given new life, and Israel will get the violent cover it needs to complete the rape of Palestine. Those are the likely outcomes of a collective failure of judgment by the United States, the European Union, Israel, and the UN. Both intended and unintended consequences are future horror stories.

Chapter 11.
Lebanon—The Israeli Game Plan

7-22-06

Yesterday the Israelis issued an injunction to all people to evacuate southern Lebanon. The Israeli instructions are to clear the coastal region of Lebanon from the Israeli border to the Litani River. The zone to be evacuated is about 25 miles deep and normally contains about 250,000 people. However, many foreigners have been evacuated through Tyre, the main city of the region, and the Lebanese population is left to its own devices to escape. At the same time, the Israel Defense Force (IDF) has massed forces on the Lebanon/Israeli frontier under an obvious plan to initiate occupation of the territory Israel has asked people to evacuate. In preparation for these moves, the IDF has been conducting air and naval artillery attacks across Lebanon that appear designed to reduce the country to rubble, rendering large parts of it uninhabitable. Several hundred people have been killed and many more have been wounded.

Terrell E Arnold

Could this carnage really be about release by Hezbollah of two captured Israeli soldiers? The answer obviously is no, unless, of course, Israeli leadership have lost their collective minds. But then, what is it about?

On the face of things, as reported by mainstream media, the immediate plan is to decimate Hezbollah, and that plan appears tacitly to be approved by the United States, Western European countries and maybe a number of Arab governments. (The Arab governments are Sunni, and Hezbollah is Shia) Somewhat more than half of the Lebanese people are Shia Muslims, and a sizeable number of the Shia are members of Hezbollah, but the Israeli attacks are being carried out against all Lebanese. At least 500,000 people have been displaced and the infrastructure to support Lebanon's approximate 4,000,000 people is being systematically destroyed. In short, as the Israelis have collectively punished all Palestinians for the existence of Hamas, the IDF is now collectively punishing all Lebanese, including the large Shia Amal community, for the presence of Hezbollah.

Such all-out war is not possible on the spur of the moment. Israel obviously has been planning such a maneuver for some time, and building its inventory of American munitions and aircraft, such as Cobra helicopters, for launch on short notice. As several commentators have noted, it only needed a pretext. The pretext was the capture of two Israeli soldiers, but the likely trigger was Hezbollah's move to help the Palestinians after weeks of IDF bombardment and harassment designed to cause the fall of Palestine's Hamas government. The Hezbollah reaction to Israeli attacks on the Palestinians was predictable. Thus, Hezbollah appears to have walked into a well-prepared Israeli trap, but there is evidence it knew what was coming and was preparing for it.

The question therefore becomes: What was the Israeli game plan before Hezbollah played into their hands? The plan must be viewed through the window of long term Israeli goals. Some Israelis have for decades sought occupation and ownership of all of Palestine. Israeli refusal to negotiate settlement of any critical issue (boundaries, compensation, right of return, Palestinian statehood, access to Jerusalem), has not been due to recalcitrance or steadfast refusal of the Palestinians to come to terms; it has been due simply to Israeli leadership refusal to give on any issue where long term Israeli interests would have to be in some way fixed, reduced, prejudiced, redefined or given away.

The opportunity presented by failure to agree on any key issue has been used repeatedly by Israel to create new facts on the ground. The Palestinians have gained nothing but accumulating losses from this process, i.e., (1) reduced Palestinian presence in Jerusalem due to de facto expulsion, (2) increased Israeli presence in the West Bank through creation of settlements and exclusive roads to reach them, (3) increasing co-option of water resources by Israelis and decreasing allocations of water to Palestinians, (4) increasing time, distance, death of parties, and erection of competing rights to

Terrell E Arnold

lands, buildings, olive trees and other valuable assets, (5) incremental shifts in boundaries due to settlements, the wandering wall and other boundary creep, (6) long term and systematic expulsion of Palestinians from their lands, villages and homes in present day Israel (7) systematic exclusion of Palestinians from the Jordan Valley, and other examples such as denial of citizenship to Palestinians who live in Israel.

If history is any guide, this same game plan would be extended to Lebanon. Note the deliberate and generalized destruction of the Lebanese infrastructure: Roads, bridges, port facilities, airport runways and buildings, urban housing and roads. The Israeli argument for these attacks is that any feature of the Lebanese infrastructure is part of a terrorism support system. But in the long run this destructive attack pattern is all designed to assure that the Lebanon that exists after a ceasefire will not be capable for a long time of any significant resistance. This plan may backfire, however, because the Syrians may decide to cross the Ante-Lebanon and Lebanon Mountains and re-enter what is left of Lebanon. Moreover, the sizeable Shia Amal population may be provoked by Israeli pounding into combining forces with Hezbollah in militant as well as in the political terms that already exist. The pattern of attack assures that Israel will have few, if any, friends in the future Lebanon.

The Israeli attack on Lebanon has revealed a pattern of double standards that may permanently change the global attack on terrorism and insurgency, if not warfare in general.

First, absent significant US, UN and European objections, the Israelis are being encouraged—at least given room—to virtually destroy Lebanon as a state. This establishes a pattern for any who care to use it of deliberate disassembly of any state that willingly or unwillingly harbors an insurgent/terrorist group. However, any other government that uses this pattern should expect sharp criticism, not the tolerant indulgence being shown Israel.

Second, the Israelis are attacking another country with American weapons in violation of US laws. While far from objecting, the US is undertaking emergency supply of smart bombs and other explosives to compound the destruction of Lebanon.

Third, the Israelis are being given free rein to destroy Lebanon and Palestine on the pretext that Hezbollah has captured two Israeli soldiers and the Palestinians have captured one. But at the same time the whole world is silent about the fact that the Israelis hold hundreds of Lebanese and thousands of Palestinians, some who have been confined for decades, but few of them have ever been charged with any specific crime or brought to trial.

Fourth, Hezbollah is being encouraged to lay down its arms and stop fighting, but the Israelis are tacitly being given enough time, by the US particularly, to complete their destruction of any Hezbollah infrastructure; if the Hezbollah forces quit now, the Israelis are likely to decimate them.

<u>Fifth</u>, Hezbollah, and implicitly the whole of Lebanon, are being charged with the sin of being supported by Syria and Iran, while it is patently OK for Israel to receive massive support from the United States, Britain and others.

Such a pattern of standards is working to polarize the planet in a manner we have never before witnessed. This is not about the traditional bi-polar collisions of great powers. This is about the rights and interests of the great majority of the world's people being abused and trampled upon by a small cluster of elites. That pattern of catering to Israeli aggression is dominated by, but is not limited to, the United States.

In the meantime, Israel has been given perfect cover for achievement of a long held goal. If the Israelis have their way, key new facts on the ground will be created in what is now southern Lebanon. Israel has had its eye on that area for decades.

The prize is the Litani River, a stream that rises in the Lebanon mountain range, flows south for more than half its length, then turns west and enters the Mediterranean some miles north of the city of Tyre. As seen from Israel, there is no other comparable potential source of potable or irrigation waters in the region other than costly desalination of the sea itself. With that river in mind, in the 1930s David Ben-Gurion, one of the founding fathers of Israel, conceived of boundaries for the fledgling state of Israel that extended from the Litani River in Lebanon across the Syrian Desert and Jordan and south into the Sinai Peninsula. Others have dreamed of the waters of the Litani and have concocted schemes such as pipelines and tunnels to bring the water to Israel. Ben-Gurion's map not only scooped up the Litani but grabbed the Yarmuk River as well, the only significant feed to the Jordan River from the Jordanian side.

In brutal terms, in a land where water is life, the Israelis are willing to kill, wound and displace many thousands of people, and remake the regional map to get more water. That pattern has preempted most of the waters of the Jordan basin, both aquifers and flowing streams for Israeli use—at the expense mainly of the Palestinians and the Jordanians.

It is clear that the Israelis now plan to take the territory and plant themselves on the banks of the Litani. That area comprises about 5% of Lebanese territory. Under the guise of ending the threat posed by Hezbollah to the northern areas of Israel, the idea will be to create a "buffer zone". As the Israelis see it, Hezbollah has underscored that necessity by successfully dropping missiles on Haifa in the current engagement.

Terrell E Arnold

The idea of a buffer zone is unlikely to be opposed by the US, the Europeans or the UN. The problem the Israelis have to solve is how to keep the buffer zone from being manned by foreign troops. Foreign troops in the zone will be no help to Israel's scheme. They must be in charge and able to create new facts on the ground that will make the occupied Lebanese territory part of Israel. That scheme has worked successfully to acquire virtually every inch of Israel at no acquisition cost to the Israelis. So why adopt any other scheme?

The starting gambit is to get the United States, the Europeans, and the UN to support Israeli occupation of the territory "for the time being", while the dust settles and the Lebanese in the rest of the country try to put their lives back together. That recovery process will take longer than the Israelis need to de facto finish annexation of south Lebanon.

If this scheme works, through yet another irrational appearing, but calculated, act of carnage, Israel will have pulled off a three part coup. It will have removed Hezbollah as a threat to Israel from Lebanon; it will have eliminated Hezbollah as a paramilitary and psychological source of support to the Palestinians; and it will have stolen the waters of the Litani River.

To initiate such a grand design, Prime Minister Ehud Olmert's strategic planners needed only an excuse to start. The Hezbollah capture of Israeli soldiers was plausible. Partly as a result of Hezbollah destruction of a US Marine barracks in Beirut in the mid-1980s, eliminating Hezbollah had resonance in the West. It can be hoped that neither reason lasts long enough to cover the Israeli plan to steal the Litani River and southern Lebanon from the Lebanese people.

Chapter 12.
Bush & Blair— Lebanon Is Not A Video Game

7-30-06

Friday President George Bush and Prime Minister Tony Blair agreed on a simplistic and video game-like solution to the conflict in Lebanon. Its main elements appear to have been: (1) The Israelis would make a creditable showing of ability to defeat Hezbollah at least to the point where, (2) Hezbollah would be willing to enter into a cease-fire and negotiations, while (3) Hezbollah would show that it knows it is being defeated; (4) demonstrate that it is prepared to disarm and, perforce, (5) allow itself to be disarmed and disassembled. And (6) that would be accomplished by the (virtually nonexistent) Lebanese army under the watchful eye, but without the direct involvement of an (as yet to be established) international force comprised of troops contributed by (as yet unnamed) UN member nations. Over the next few days, maybe weeks, this was to be a neatly worked out scenario in which everybody knew their roles, and nobody stumbled over the script.

Terrell E Arnold

The key problem may have been that the co-belligerents were not involved in designing the script. The Israelis probably were consulted behind the scenes, but Hezbollah most likely was not. However, element one of the game clearly meant that the Israelis would be given more time—at least several more days—to make the demonstration that they could defeat Hezbollah.

But things other than warfare and not in the game-plan were developing rapidly on the ground and in the region. Hezbollah was acquiring popularity, even among Sunnis in the region that suggested it could easily displace al Qaida as the leader of insurgency in Islam. At home, Hezbollah was also gaining a new respect among the Lebanese and that popularity (over 70% of all Lebanese in one poll) was moving Lebanese politics visibly toward some new configuration.

That new configuration burst on the scene Saturday when Hezbollah agreed with a Lebanese proposal for a cease-fire which the Israelis promptly dismissed. Element 1 in the Bush/Blair scheme prevailed because the Israelis suggested the Hezbollah willingness to halt the fighting meant they were losing. Therefore, the Israeli desire was to fight on to see if they could finish off Hezbollah. Bush and Blair appear also to have favored fighting on, and they refused to agree to a cease-fire until Hezbollah was, in effect, defeated and disarmed.

Perhaps encouraging that position, there was no mention in the Lebanese proposal that Hezbollah

PALESTINE In Need of a Just God

would give up its arms. Avoiding such issues, Kofi Annan called essentially for a truce to deal with the woeful human conditions of the combat zone and surroundings, as well as to bring in the as yet non-existent international force.

Then, in its eagerness to defeat Hezbollah, the IDF repeated a tragic blunder. Early Sunday morning the IDF bombed an apartment house in Qana, the UN base near the Israel/Lebanon border. The building was destroyed and more than 50 refugees, most of them children, were killed. Israel had conducted a bombing raid on this UN facility a decade earlier, killing more than 100 people. The Bush/Blair video game came apart because the real players in the conflict were not playing their parts in the game; they were acting out their own roles on the ground.

That condition sums up the nature of the whole situation in the Middle East today. A cease-fire may indeed emerge in Lebanon in the next several days, but, unless the Bush/Blair video game is modified to include Palestine, any cease-fire will affect less than half of the current Middle East conflict. The rest is occurring without notice in Palestine, really in Gaza, where the Israelis are making a full court press to defeat the Palestinians—read destroy Hamas—once and for all.

If Bush and Blair addressed this part of the present Israeli shooting war, there is no evidence of it in the media reports on their meetings. The absence of that conflict on their negotiating table heightens the video gaming quality of their discourse. They appear to have been discussing Lebanon as if it were in a vacuum. The fact is that Hezbollah is in much of its trouble because of its efforts to help the Palestinian people, and Sheikh Hassan Nasrallah surely knows full well what is happening in Gaza under cover of the Lebanon conflict. He therefore is likely to give some thought to what will happen if the IDF becomes free to turn its full power loose on the Palestinians.

Failure to include the raging conflict in Palestine in the terms of any proposed cease-fire or stand-down places the United States squarely in the Israeli camp on the whole regional conflict. Earlier in the week, Secretary Rice reportedly visited Ramallah to pay a call on Mahmud Abbas, pointedly demonstrating that the US is still trying to ignore the Hamas Government and hasten its downfall. Perhaps because of that objective, she neither visited Gaza nor appears to have mentioned Gaza in any of her comments about efforts to resolve the conflict. She is said now to be in Jerusalem, working on a cease-fire proposal, but the real effect of the time she spends there gives the IDF more time to act as it did this morning at Qana.

The Palestine part of the conflict thus joins the long history of US indifference to what is daily happening to the Palestinian people. But it also underscores the video game character of US and British designs for resolving the Lebanon conflict. They seem to want to resolve it without touching—or even mentioning—the core problem of the Middle East, Palestinian repression by the Israelis. With or without deliberation, the scheme to give the IDF more time to defeat and disarm Hezbollah is giving the IDF ideal cover for continuing their effort in Gaza to destroy the remainder of the Palestinian will to resist.

The judgments of several experienced Middle East observers, who prefer to be nameless, are that the IDF, the Olmert government and its backers in the US and elsewhere, will not succeed on either front. While Hezbollah may be experiencing increasing combat problems on the ground in Lebanon, its position in Islamic society has soared, and, therefore, its capacities to raise recruits and resources have multiplied. At the same time, without necessarily realizing that or having that as an objective, Hezbollah has become a more potent political force in Lebanon.

Meanwhile, the Palestinians, especially those in Gaza, are being collectively punished for the refusal of some of their members to stop fighting back and for their collective decision to elect Hamas. In truth, Hamas and Hezbollah now represent the principal defenders of the Palestinians, and that may be reinforced in the future as the result of the Lebanon conflict.

The final departure from the tidiness of a video game is likely to be significant changes in future patterns of international terrorism. Both the number and

Terrell E Arnold

the severity of attacks by terrorists or insurgents are likely to increase in coming months and years. While the effort of the supporters of the IDF attack on Lebanon may have been directed at getting rid of a single insurgent group, the consequences over time may well be that the group itself grows stronger, and the numbers of other such groups are likely to increase.

Not only in Lebanon, but in yet unknown times and places, among them certainly Israel, the violent fruits of the misbegotten Lebanon enterprise will be harvested. None of those future tragedies appear in the video game scenario played out by Bush and Blair. Most of them can be deflected, if the United States, Britain, Israel, the Europeans, the UN and indeed everyone else recognize the abiding tragedy that is Palestine, and recognize that the core problem underlying much of the unrest in the region and elsewhere is the persecution of the Palestinians by Israel.

There simply is no chance that a cease-fire confined to Lebanon will do any good beyond stopping the destruction of Lebanon by Israel. Any peace plan that does not recognize the core problem of Palestine is doomed to fail, because Lebanon is not the problem; the Lebanese Shia are not the problem; Syria is not the problem; Iran is not the problem; Israeli repression of the Palestinian people is the problem. A game plan that does not recognize these realities is fit only for a PlayStation.

Chapter 13.
The IDF Should Do The Numbers

8-3-06

In the past few days, Israel's IDF has begun moving deeper into Lebanon. While Israeli announcements of this plan did not include details, the goal is to clear the area of south Lebanon up to the Litani River of any Hezbollah fighters. Israeli officials have said that already some 300 of an estimated 2,000 Hezbollah fighters have been killed. According to a New York Times report, Brigadier General Shakar of Israel's Northern Command indicated that the IDF is forming a "Red Line" along both sides of the Litani River—which runs pretty much east to west after it leaves the Lebanon range—and that a force amounting to around six brigades or 10,000 men would be fielded for this task. An overall objective, according to the Times, is to clear a two to three mile wide zone of land north of the Lebanon-Israel frontier of all Hezbollah fighters, explosives, mines, outposts, storage areas, barracks and other infrastructure, so that an international force can be deployed there without itself having to engage Hezbollah.

Terrell E Arnold

Couched in the jargon of military maneuver, the plan sounds plausible. However, the numbers are, to say the least, challenging. As a practical matter, delivery on the plan would require a scorched earth sterilization of several hundred square miles of southern Lebanon, while maintaining effective occupation of roughly 75-100 square miles of Lebanon to north of the Litani River. That averages out to less than 20 men per square mile. Such a force is equivalent to a decent hunting or foraging party, but hardly a substantial fighting force when scattered over the whole region.

The rejoinder to that observation is likely to be: But those forces will be assembled into fighting units according to the needs of identified battle zones. Right, as Sun Tzu or Clausewitz might say, but where is the battle? Here guerrilla warfare, as practiced by Hezbollah, has proven to be a baffling ordeal. After three weeks Israelis are asking why the best army in the region, the one that beat three national armies in six days, has been unable to beat a ragtag bunch of insurgents in three weeks. The second embarrassing question is: Having bombed poor Lebanon for several weeks with impunity, without resistance, and with the best equipment on the planet, why hasn't the IDF found and destroyed the battlefield?

Here the IDF really needs to do the numbers. To start with, how many Hezbollah are there? At last count (estimate), Lebanon had almost 4 million people. Roughly 60% of the population is Islamic. An estimated 40% of the population is Shi'a, and roughly half (who knows exactly) of the Shi'a population appears to be Hezbollah. In effect, that means as many as 20-25% of the Lebanese (800,000-1,000,000 people) could be associated with Hezbollah. However, clouding that number even more is the fact that recent polls indicate that as many as 80-85% of all Lebanese now strongly favor Hezbollah.

Both of the above percentage sets pose major problems for engaging a guerrilla war in Lebanon. The State Department estimates Hezbollah fighting strength at "several thousand," while the International Institute for Strategic Studies suggests the fighting force, including actives, backups and reserves, could exceed 15-20,000. Even if the fighting element of Hezbollah is on the low side of those numbers, the asymmetrical nature of guerrilla war, the ease with which such forces can hide in and receive support from the general population, and the fact that battle grounds are more than likely to be chosen by Hezbollah than by the IDF, would commend a much larger force than Israel has deployed or has talked about. Meanwhile, interdicting Hezbollah re-supply, not only from Iran and Syria but offshore sources, is a major challenge, and the Lebanese know their coast line and mountains far better than the Israelis.

The numbers suggest that a prudent Israeli/US objective would be to stop soon and not risk the likely failure of an effort to eliminate Hezbollah as a fighting force. At the moment, the prospect is for a war that will be very costly in Israeli blood and treasure, to say noth-

Terrell E Arnold

ing of the costs to Lebanon. Standoff and other bombing operations will not take care of this. The most likely outcome appears little better than a draw. And that says nothing of the political furor in Lebanon, Israel, the United States and the rest of the world that will be generated by an Israeli effort to sterilize southern Lebanon by the gross means it already has applied to Lebanon as a whole.

Chapter 14.
US-French Ceasefire Agreement Not Good Enough

8-6-06

According to Associated Press reports, the United States and France agreed Friday on the terms of a UN Security Council resolution to end the fighting in Lebanon. The main thrust of the agreed language is an awkwardly worded call for an "immediate cessation by Hezbollah of all attacks and the immediate cessation by Israel of all offensive military operations." This language is said to permit Israel to defend itself if attacked, but if the deal is strictly followed, Hezbollah would not be permitted to fight back if the Israelis attacked alleging self-defense.

The overall thrust of the proposed resolution would be to create a system for working around Hezbollah in Lebanon. While Israel appears to have been consulted on the terms—hence the language permitting self-defense—there have been no indications that Hezbollah was or would be a party to the agreement. Rather, the

Terrell E Arnold

government of Lebanon would be assigned the task of disarming Hezbollah, and Lebanon would agree to and enforce rules on the acquisition of arms and ammunition that would be designed to prevent Hezbollah from importing them from abroad, e.g., from Syria or Iran.

This resolution would create a buffer zone between Israel and Lebanon that extends from the present border region some 20-25 miles into Lebanon to the north side of the Litani River. The resolution would provide for delineating the Israeli-Lebanese border, notably clearing up the problem of the Lebanese territory known as Shebaa Farms that the Israelis captured in 1967 and held onto when they withdrew from Lebanon in 2000.

The present UN force, UNIFIL, would monitor the end of hostilities. Once the Israelis and Lebanon agree on the principles, the UN Security Council would authorize a new peacekeeping force which would have the mission to "support the Lebanese armed forces and government in providing a secure environment and contribute to the implementation of a permanent cease-fire and a long term solution." This formulation gives Israel the means to delay fielding of an international force indefinitely, simply by refusing to agree to principles proposed by Hezbollah or the Lebanese government. Thus, if implemented in those terms, the cease-fire could give Israel extended occupation of the area south of the Litani River.

PALESTINE In Need of a Just God

It will be interesting to see how this plays in Lebanon. The first problem with it is that there is no stated intent to include any representative of Hezbollah in the process. Hezbollah is about to be asked by Lebanese officials to disarm, but, overtly at least, it is being offered nothing for such a concession. Something of value would be guaranteed freedom from capricious attack, including targeted assassination, by Israeli forces in southern Lebanon and/or agents elsewhere such as in the Biqaa Valley. That would prohibit such Israeli incursions as the raid that led to the capture by Hezbollah of the two Israeli IDF soldiers inside Lebanon.

Something of value would be recognition that the Lebanese Shia, including Hezbollah and Shia Amal, are roughly half of Lebanon's population, the majority of its Muslims, and full participants in the Lebanese political process. Nabih Berri, the long-time head of Shia Amal and speaker of the Lebanese Parliament, appears to be acting for Hezbollah leader Sheikh Hasan Nasrallah and speaking for Lebanon in rejecting the US-French proposal. He says the proposal is short by at least seven points. The required terms include (1) an immediate cease-fire, (2) withdrawal of Israeli troops from Lebanon, (3) an immediate prisoner exchange (Hezbollah has two Israeli prisoners, the Israelis hold hundreds, maybe thousands of Lebanese prisoners.), (4) takeover of control in the south by Lebanese forces, (5) fielding of an international force at the present Israeli-Lebanese frontier, (6) return of displaced Lebanese to their home areas, and (7) provision of an Israeli map of minefields left over from the previous Israeli occupation. Phase one of this plan would be immediate action on points 1-3.

The Berri proposal does not address key issues in the US-French plan: The disarmament of Hezbollah and arrangements to prevent its re-formation or rearmament, as well as formation of a Lebanese force that (it appears) would not include Hezbollah fighters. This is a complex political corner for both Prime Minister Siniora and Nabih Berri. They have avoided these issues in the Lebanese proposal because they know that such actions, if attempted, risk reviving civil war in Lebanon, the reopening of Muslim/Christian divisions that have plagued Lebanon for centuries, including most of the past twenty years. Given the new-found popularity of Hezbollah leader Nasrallah among Lebanese generally, actions to ignore or discredit Hezbollah could well cause the present government to fall, while re-igniting such divisions.

Neither plan appears overtly to recognize that Nasrallah, as leader of Hezbollah, is also the leader of an important political party in Lebanon, a cleric of renown among Shia Muslims, and has growing stature among Muslims of both Shia and Sunni persuasions worldwide. Thus, for many Muslims, the failure to involve him personally in the settlement of this dispute would be the first sign that the drafters of a UN Security Council resolution do not really understand or care what has been going on here as the Muslim world sees it.

PALESTINE In Need of a Just God

The US-French proposal misses an important opportunity. Hezbollah always has been primarily political in its focus. Its broad public service and public works performance in southern Lebanon is the root of its popularity among Lebanese Muslims; that, plus the fact that it is fighting Israel and the West in defense of Muslims and their values. Negotiation of a peace in Lebanon is a chance to move Hezbollah more decisively toward its political role. In the past few years it already has moved to a political position strong enough to hold two ministerial posts in the present government and to share political power equally with Shia Amal. While Israel may not like that, folding Hezbollah fighters legally into the Lebanese military force would both increase the capabilities of Lebanese forces to defend themselves and bring Hezbollah forces under the law, at least notionally constraining their actions against Israel.

In fact, ignoring the main elements of the Lebanese proposal, while failing to engage Nasrallah directly in the process of terminating the war in Lebanon, will label the peace as a connivance of outsiders who recognize none of the rights and interests of anyone other than Israel and the United States. That alone will make the peace fragile, and probably temporary, to say the least.

Chapter 15.
The Israeli/American Terrorism Generator

11-5-06

For more than half a century, the Israelis have billed themselves in America as the innocent victims of Palestinian terrorism. And the United States has assiduously defended the Israeli right of "self-defense", most aggressively by vetoing at least 35 UN Security Council resolutions that were in some way critical of Israel. The most recent would have called on Israel to terminate its present destructive military campaign in Gaza. Those vetoes received little attention in American media, and as is becoming much better known in recent months, the truth about Israel's virtual genocide of the Palestinian people has simply been denied to most Americans. It is not only time that changed; it is also time Americans in general understood the consequences for their safety and America's reputation of this decades long perversion of American foreign policy.

Starting in a big way with the Israeli terrorist massacre of the villagers of Deir Yassin in 1947, the pressure on Palestinians to leave Palestine, to voluntarily give up their homes and historic ties, with no hope of return or compensation, has been unremitting. That has been true even in periods when alleged peace processes were at work, because the average Palestinian was simply never permitted to see any genuine prospect of peace or a national home. Rather, the most persistent element of Israeli policy toward Palestinians is to deny them either security or peace.

Since the beginning of the George W. Bush administration, Israeli creation of unremitting hopelessness has been allowed steadily to accelerate. The Second Intifada—actually open rebellion of Palestinians against continuing Israeli oppression—was nominally triggered by Ariel Sharon's 2000 visit to the Temple Mount, the site of the Muslim Dome of the Rock and the al Aqsa Mosque, but real triggers were economic discontent and recognition by Palestinians generally that the "peace process" was going nowhere. That was followed by systematic disassembly of the Palestinian infrastructure by the occupying Israel Defense Force, one of the most egregious examples being total destruction of the village of Jenin in 2002. That was followed by George W. Bush's agreement with Sharon that new settlements in the West Bank were "facts on the ground" to be taken into account—meaning stolen land added to Israel—in any future peace negotiation.

The Al Aqsa Martyrs Brigades took their name and their style from the perceived Sharon insult to Islam represented by his visit to the Temple Mount. The

Brigades, for a time, became the bloodiest of Palestinian insurgents, mostly through attacks on Israel. Other Palestinian groups, Hamas for example, were also active in this period, and Israel, as well as effectively the Bush administration, used violent Palestinian resistance as an excuse for continued repression. There is no other conflict on the Planet at this time that feeds consciously and deliberately on the fact that people who are oppressed regularly and harshly enough will fight back.

Slowly but unremittingly the Palestinians are being squeezed into an area of the West Bank and the Gaza strip that amounts to less than 10% of Palestine, and new "facts on the ground" add daily to the Israeli numbers: The 90% consists of Israel (by UN definition the territory enclosed by the 1967 truce line) the expanding blocks of settlements pre-approved by George W. Bush, the Israeli-only roads being built to reach them, the encroaching Israeli wall designed to create a boundary fact on the ground, and denial to Palestinian entry or use of the whole of the Jordan River Valley.

All of that has been playing out since January 2006 in a political environment dominated by the US/Israeli effort to starve Hamas out of power if not altogether out of existence in Palestine. Under the growing pressure of declining resources, inadequate electric power, an open prison and oppressive situation for virtually all Palestinians, the people are beginning to squabble. Under the conditions of Palestine, the struggle to survive, perversely allied with the desire to find someone to blame for adversity, will cause people to fight among themselves.

That was the state of play as of July-August 2006. In September, more or less simultaneously with their invasion of Lebanon, the Israelis upped the pressure. The box score at this time is the Palestinians have one Israeli prisoner, while the Israelis hold 9,000 or more Palestinians. Nevertheless, ostensibly in response to Palestinian kidnapping of an Israeli soldier—actually capture in Palestinian territory after an Israeli assault failed—the IDF launched an all-out campaign to unseat Hamas and, once and for all, to squelch any Palestinian idea of their own state. This campaign was launched under the international media cover of the Israeli invasion of Lebanon. It has continued without interruption or any US action to restrain it, even through a visit of Secretary of State Condoleezza Rice to meet with Mahmoud Abbas in September.

As the world saw, the Lebanon campaign was harsh, devastating to many areas of the country, heavily destructive of the national infrastructure, and it was actively fed with weapons by the US as well as prolonged by US/British refusal to push an immediate ceasefire. As the world also saw, the stated purpose of the Israeli campaign in Lebanon, to capture, kill or disband the Shia group Hezbollah, was a failure. Hezbollah lives, to fight on, and the prospect that it will be disbanded or disarmed is slight, while its popularity as a defender of

PALESTINE In Need of a Just God

Islamic causes has grown remarkably. That probably has encouraged numerous insurgencies.

Meanwhile, Israel's IDF has continued its harsh campaign against the Palestinians, especially in the Gaza Strip, and it has done so with little to no objection from the international community. In fact, both Israeli leadership and the Bush administration continue to hope that this campaign will result in the collapse of the Hamas Government and return of power to Mahmoud Abbas of Yasser Arafat's Fatah movement—that to be followed by renewal of a peace process. That process will go nowhere, because present Israeli leadership will simply not let it go anywhere, and Israel's main sponsor, the United States, remains disinclined to intervene.

At least some Israelis and their Jewish supporters in the United States and elsewhere know that this situation is a disaster in the making. The Israeli hardliners, meaning the Zionists most devoted to a Jewish state, must hope that under the pressures now being exerted the Palestinians will go away. The newest member of Olmert's government, Avigdor Lieberman of the extremist Israel Beiteinu party, advocates forcibly making the Palestinians leave any area of Palestine west of the Jordan River. Moreover, his inclusion in the Olmert government was virtually unanimous, and that means hardly anyone in the Olmert government wants a renewed peace process with the Palestinians.

The only clear winners in the present Palestine situation are the Middle Eastern and international promoters of terrorism. Trackers of the history of the Palestinian conflict will recall that increasing Israeli oppression of the Palestinian people in the 1960s brought on Yasser Arafat's creation of the PLO, the Palestine Liberation Organization. Washington terrorism experts, one of whom—during the 1980s and 1990s—was this writer, if honest with themselves, will also admit that constant US defense and support of Israel provoked much of the anti-US terrorism of those and later years. Continued repression of the Palestinians through the 1970s and 1980s brought on spin-offs from the PLO such as the Popular Front for the Liberation of Palestine, the PFLP General Command, and Islamic activists such as Palestinian Islamic Jihad. The first Palestinian Intifada in the late 1980s brought on the emergence of Hamas, while the Second Intifada, as noted earlier, brought on creation of the Al Aqsa Martyrs Brigades.

The present Israeli campaign—at least as intensive and repressive as any earlier assault on the Palestinians—is likely to spawn one or more new groups. No one is likely to know in advance who they are; they won't necessarily be Palestinian; they may not necessarily even be Islamic.

Their targets will find out who they are (maybe) and what they want (maybe) only when they strike. The fact is that Israeli leadership, bent on a once-for-all solution to its Palestine problem, has turned up the Middle East terrorism generator to full flame. By not strenuously objecting to the Israeli campaign in Palestine, and

PALESTINE In Need of a Just God

by force-feeding the Israeli campaign in Lebanon, the United States has added its own fuel to this terrorism igniter.

It may be too late to turn this flame down or off. It may be that there are actually people in Washington and Tel Aviv who revel in the thought they can count on a "reliable" set of enemies for their wars on terrorism. In this respect, Israel has been its own worst enemy for more than half a century. The United States has joined that club by actively helping to make war on Palestinian leadership. By their hostile interventions in Palestine, both are asking to be the targets of groups that may not be large, but who will be determined, and the War on Terrorism will not be able to stop them.

Chapter 16.
The Partners to War Crime in the Holy Land

12-27-06

With growing force Western and Islamic country critics are charging that Israeli treatment of the Palestinian people is an ongoing war crime. Ever more clearly the fact is coming into the open that Israel is not alone in carrying out this crime, but is aided and abetted in financial, legal, material and spiritual ways that mount quickly toward direct involvement of outsiders in the crime. In effect, Israeli abuse, persecution, confiscation of property, denial of rights, and outright murder of Palestinians has morphed into an international war crime.

In November the Israel Defense Force (IDF) massacred 18 people in the Gaza community of Beit Hanoun. Most of them were women and children as well as senior citizens. President Bush expressed his regrets at the killings, but the US vetoed a UN Security Council resolution seeking to stop Israeli military operations, to investigate the Beit Hanoun killings, and to call on Israel to

Terrell E Arnold

comply with the Geneva Conventions. Ten members of the Security Council voted for the resolution, while four permanent members (China, France, Russia, and Britain—the other owners of a veto power) abstained. European media mostly decried the Beit Hanoun incident as just another unfortunate episode in the ongoing Israeli occupation of Palestine. If the story made the front pages of any newspapers, it quickly faded from sight.

In the meantime, IDF targeted killings of Palestinians and destruction of homes and businesses continued uninterrupted. As a de facto announcement of intent, Israel has established border posts on the Jordan Valley frontier with Jordan, forcibly annexing this large piece of the West Bank into Israel. No public objection to this blatant act of confiscating Palestinian lands has been made by Jordan, the United States, or by the UN which, because of US Security Council vetoes, cannot effectively record what its member states might think. In short, the ongoing war crime designed to disrupt and destroy any remaining Palestinian society, confiscate all Palestinian lands, and kill, confine or dislocate any Palestinians, armed or unarmed, goes on unimpeded by any international moral or legal authority.

Israel claims that IDF forces occupy Palestine to protect Israelis. On the average IDF forces kill, imprison or dispossess hundreds of Palestinians for any one Israeli who is killed or injured. However, the outside world, principally Western nations, buy (at least do not challenge) the Israeli excuse that they are acting in self-

PALESTINE In Need of a Just God

defense. The gross double standard involved is crystal clear in the facts of the present Israeli assault. The Israelis hold more than 9,000 Palestinians prisoner, mostly without any charge, but Palestinian resistance to that condition through lobbing primitive rockets into Israel is called "terrorism", while Palestinian militant capture of one soldier appears accepted by the international community as a sufficient excuse for IDF forces to carry out a virtual scorched earth program in Gaza.

This body of crime, altered over the decades only by Israeli acquisition of newer weapons, began before the state of Israel was recognized by President Harry Truman in 1948. In anticipation that such a state would be created and at least eventually recognized, Israel's Zionist founders already had formed terrorist groups to acquire the land needed to make that state a reality. Starting immediately with the massacre and forcible expulsion of the villagers of Deir Yassin, these groups (Stern and Irgun and the follow-up Haganah) began the systematic clearing of Palestinians village by village, emptying hundreds of communities of clans and families who had lived there for centuries to make way for newly-arriving Israelis, and eventually their sons and daughters.

That systematic confiscation of Palestine from its people, once begun, has yet to stop. No peace process, however widely touted, has interrupted the Israeli land grab. Today creeping settlement building, a meandering wall and forceful denial of Jordan Valley access to

Terrell E Arnold

Palestinians daily confiscate new acreage to the expanding state of Israel.

On Christmas Day 2006, it is deeply troubling to see what this Israeli campaign has done to the most sacred of Christian sites, the "little town of Bethlehem." Because it was the birthplace of Jesus, Bethlehem, a present-day town of 28,000, is the oldest continuously inhabited site of Christendom and for that reason has been the most frequently visited by pilgrims and tourists.

Today people cannot get into Bethlehem or out of it. As reported by a Palestinian Christian (See Ray Hanania in the Arab American News and on rense.com) the town is surrounded in part by the meandering Israeli wall that cuts the town off from Jerusalem; travel is impeded by razor wire barricades, roadblocks and checkpoints that impede not only the movements of visitors but the daily lives and movements of the Palestinian people; the Biblical site of Rachel's Tomb has been surrounded by Israeli forces, while Israeli settlements take over the surrounding hills. Palestinian Christians, whose lineages often go back to ancient times, are trapped, unable to move in or out and barely able to practice their faith. Not only the Biblical site of the birthplace of Jesus but also the surrounding lands—<u>among the best watered in the West Bank</u>—is being confiscated by the Israelis. And that process of steady expulsion of the Palestinians continues while Israelis bluster about their need to defend themselves against people they daily seek to destroy.

PALESTINE In Need of a Just God

Before the eyes of the world the oldest continuing war crime on the planet—more than six decades of it—progresses unopposed except by Palestinians who fight back and are called terrorists for doing so. A war crime of this magnitude—the Israeli confiscation of roughly 90% of Palestine and willful displacement, slaughter, imprisonment, and prison camp confinement of Palestinians now numbering over four million—cannot go on without help from outside.

Israel receives a great deal of help. Jewish financial groups, communities, and individuals worldwide have poured money into the venture, while governments, mainly western and principally the United States, have kept Israel solvent while it used its armed force, the Israel Defense Force (IDF) to fend off angered Palestinians, to protect land stealing settlers, and to confiscate more land for Greater Israel. The white European Ashkenazi Jews, who perpetrate this crime, as well as their white Christian right supporters of the George W. Bush presidency, seem totally indifferent to the ongoing Israeli repression of the native peoples of Palestine. The fact that those Palestinian Christians, Muslims and Jews are descended from the people of the book—Semitic peoples of Palestine—appears to give them little weight in the Zionist or Christian right conscience.

While its treatment of the Palestinians made Israel a pariah in the Muslim world, early on in this process, Israeli leadership figured out how to protect its status as a nation state. Israel achieved virtual immunity from criticism, by assuring through political bribery and spurious charges of "anti-Semitism" that its crime would go un-remarked and unpunished, if not unnoticed.

Those tools also assured that Israel (a) would become the single largest recipient of US aid (40 to 50% or more of total US foreign assistance each year), (b) would be the recipient of even larger annual loans that regularly are forgiven—in short, donations, (c) would have no strings attached to its receipt of US assistance, and (d) would be protected from international objections to its behavior by US veto of any UN Security Council attempts to criticize or moderate Israeli actions.

With the bulk of its remaining annual foreign aid package, the United States also buys the general silence of Jordan and Egypt, pretty much no matter what Israel does to the Palestinian people. Subject to the same political bribery as the White House and the rest of the Executive, the Congress goes along with this program, although there is said to be plenty of cloakroom griping and contempt for it among members of Congress.

The enduring tragedy of this situation is that it has become a war crime with no end in sight short of total dispossession and expulsion of the Palestinian people. The harsh truth of it, however, is that this crime persists because it is widely shared. Europeans and many other nations have a hand in it because they have not objected seriously enough to Israeli behavior to moderate it. Middle Eastern states have helped the Palestinians financially from time to time but have not exerted forceful enough pressure on other governments to pressure Israel into stopping.

The United States, however, is a willing and complicit participant in the war crime. Putting aside likely reflex protests, let us look at the facts. Start with the 1948 US recognition of the new state of Israel, even though the expulsion of Palestinians had already begun. Track a pattern of five decades of US defense of misbehaving Israelis. Jump to last summer's Israeli invasion of Lebanon. While the United States supplied weapons for Israeli efforts to achieve a decisive victory against Hezbollah, and Israel's air force used the time virtually to destroy the Lebanese infrastructure, the US completely ignored the fact that a similar scorched earth assault was being conducted against the Palestinians in Gaza. That assault, which led to the Beit Hanoun massacre, continues undiminished.

Meanwhile, the United States and Israel are attempting to starve the Palestinian people into unseating their Hamas-led government, freely and fairly elected though it be. More directly, there is little doubt that without US aid grants and loans, as well as supplies, Israel's IDF would be unable to pursue its harassment of the Palestinians.

But the bottom line US contribution to this war crime is allowing the Israelis freely to use US-supplied military helicopters and other weapons to harass, confine, assassinate, and control the Palestinian people. US arms export control regulations prohibit such uses of American weapons, and there is no Israeli exception to them. There is no doubt that if US funds and weapons were prohibited for such uses by the Israelis, it would become difficult if not impossible for the IDF to continue the crime.

If US authorities were to discover that any other government was financing like attacks by a terrorist group, the outcry would be immediate. In this case, the US objects regularly to supplies of weapons and other support to the Palestinians by Iran and Syria, while remaining unmoved by criticism of US weapons and financial support for Israel's IDF.

The Arms Export Control Act (Public Law 90-829) says that U.S. weapons, whether given or sold to a foreign country, can be used only for "internal security" and "legitimate self-defense". Use of U.S. weapons against civilians is prohibited. While generally looking the other way as Israel repeatedly uses US weapons against civilians, little specific exception has been taken to such extremes as use of US made bulldozers and gunships to destroy the town of Jenin, or use of a US made bulldozer to kill a young American protester, Rachel Corrie. It is hard to get exact numbers, but since the beginning of 2000, over 4,000 Palestinians have been killed by the Israelis, while fewer than 400 Israelis have been killed by Palestinians. The Israeli deaths receive mainstream media coverage in the US. Palestinian deaths seldom do.

PALESTINE In Need of a Just God

More than any previous President, George W. Bush is supported by the American Christian right. Strong believers in the message of Daniel concerning the end of days, the Christian right is avidly pro-Zionist, meaning that nothing Israel does is likely to be criticized by them, while they politically support US financial and military backing of the state of Israel. The lack of outcry from the Christian right, and its strong support for Bush in his unitary support for Israel make the Christian right a party to Israeli war crime, because they do not attempt to stop the willful abuse of the Palestinians in places such as Bethlehem, and that includes Palestinian Christians.

The UN, while on numerous occasions trying to rein in the Israelis and obtain some justice for the Palestinians, has been turned into a eunuch on Palestine by US vetoes. Those vetoes regularly protect Israel from the international political, legal and moral implications of their abuse of the Palestinians. Those vetoes in effect assure that Israel has a free hand to act as it chooses toward the people of the West Bank and Gaza. US vetoes are cast in such a form that the UN can make no criticism of Israel without making a balancing criticism of the Palestinians. Under those rules, for the past six decades the Israelis have steadily pushed the Palestinian people out of their ancestral homes and lands without being held accountable.

The newest chapters of the ongoing war crime against Palestine are being written by the political squeeze imposed by US and Israeli attempts to starve the Hamas government into submission. That squeeze—essentially denial of funding, including the Palestinian Authority's own money now held by Israel—is supported in varying degrees by the UN, by Britain and European countries, and its goal is to punish the Palestinian people for electing a government the outside world does not like. But the squeeze is only part of the outside support for Israeli war crime.

The crime is aided and abetted by a rigorous double standard. The negotiating posture of the whole western world plus Israel is that the Palestinian people must accept the situation completely and stop fighting. Arab governments, all of which actually disagree with what Israel is doing, have found no effective way to deter a nuclear armed Israel. Thus, the Palestinians must recognize Israel's right to exist, honor all past peace "agreements" or proposals, disarm Palestinian militants, and, in effect, accept continuing Israeli occupation and repression. But the Israelis are not required to concede anything in advance or to change their behavior in any way.

In this manner, Israel's Zionist leadership has cozened the outside world into helping them finish the job they began with the Balfour Declaration of 1917: Take all of Palestine to form a Jewish state. Under the Israel-tolerant rules now applied by leading governments, there is no prospect that the Zionists will be stopped from confiscating Palestinian land or harassing, killing, imprisoning and otherwise coercing the Palestinian people to give up.

If the outside world continues to go along with this process, the final chapter of this war crime will be written as the Israelis create more "facts on the ground" by simply taking more land wherever Israeli settlers want it. The elements of a viable two state solution to the Arab-Israeli crisis existed only so long as lands divided along the 1967 green line made that physically feasible. Major settlement incursions since the beginning of the George W. Bush administration have made that virtually impossible, as the Israelis define "possible".

There now seem to be two options: A single state solution could be adopted under which European Jews and Palestinians of all persuasions live in peace together. That solution appears acceptable to many Palestinians and many Jews. However, present Zionist preferences are for a Jewish state. The Zionist preferred alternative would require expelling or otherwise removing even the present non-Jewish citizens as well as all Palestinians. In short, the Zionists would prefer to carry their war crime to its ultimate conclusion: all of Palestine without Palestinians. To the extent that the Western and Arab states permit this to happen, they will all be guilty of the war crime of destroying Palestine, while ceding the Holy Land to Zionists who care naught for Christendom or Islam.

Chapter 17.
Palestine—Peace Not Apartheid
A Review

1-17-07

Palestine long has been a complex and poorly understood land and problem for most Americans. For practicing Christians it is perhaps hopelessly entangled in the Biblical character and sanctity of the Holy Land. For Americans in general the often concocted victimization of the Israeli people is common media fare. But the truly dire circumstances of the 4 plus million Palestinians, herded like cattle by the Israelis into open prisons in the Gaza Strip and the West Bank region of the Jordan River, are rarely explained to Americans. Nor are the thousands of refugees still resident in the refugee camps such as Sabra and Shatila in Lebanon and numerous camps in other countries. Thus, in the United States it has been easy for media to portray all Palestinians as terrorists and all Israelis as innocent victims of terrorism. The United States is most often purveyed in this context as an honest broker whose actions are essential to bringing the parties to successful peace negotiations, but the truth, when faced, casts America in a less helpful and even sinister light. Few Americans have been prepared to talk or write truthfully about this situation, and Zionists as well as supporters of Israel have castigated any who dare to tell it like it is.

Former President Jimmy Carter's book, <u>Palestine—Peace Not Apartheid</u>, was put to the largely uninformed American public late last year, and it had immediate impact. The book rose quickly to the top and now holds at number nine on the best seller list. That meteoric rise may have been aided by the work of two American academics, John Mearsheimer and Steven Walt whose book, <u>The Israel Lobby and US Foreign Policy</u>, was a rude awakening to many about Israel's extreme influence on American leadership and policy. Carter's book, however, stands tall on its own as a candid and authoritative commentary on Palestine and Israel's relations with each other and with their neighbors.

No other American is positioned as well as Jimmy Carter to write such a book. Even during his years as Governor of Georgia in the early 1970s, through travel to Israel and meetings with key leaders, Carter began to take on board the convoluted nature of US relations with the Middle East. As President, he became deeply troubled by the situation and took upon himself the task to find solutions. For an American President, he took the virtually unthinkable step of closeting himself with Anwar Sadat of Egypt and Menachem Begin, the 6th Prime Minister of Israel, for more than two weeks at Camp David. The result was a body of agreements, now known as the Camp David Accords, which—with

PALESTINE In Need of a Just God

UN Security Council Resolutions 242 and 338—are the basis of subsequent efforts to find peace in the Middle East.

In part due to Israeli refusal to make any vital concessions to the Palestinians, and in part due to Palestinian resort to terrorist violence, peace was not achieved as a result of those Herculean efforts. However, Jimmy Carter never gave up, and he still has not given up. As his book relates, Carter has tracked closely and often has been consulted or involved in every peacemaking effort since Camp David. He is thus a unique senior American with more than a thirty year record of close involvement in the Middle East peace process; in effect, he is the only American personally equipped to write this book.

Through Carter's eyes the reader of <u>Palestine—Peace Not Apartheid</u> will gain a view of the modest achievements and depressing failures of the peace process up to the weeks following Israel's invasion of Lebanon in July 2006. While conceding the right of Palestinians to defend their rights and interests, Carter condemns all acts of Palestinian terrorism. In this he joins the common western habit of insisting the Palestinians should not fight back against their oppressors. He is equally clear in condemning Israeli land grabs, theft of water resources, the imprisoning Israeli wall, the constant Israeli harassment and mistreatment of the Palestinians. Carter equates the sum of that Israeli misconduct toward the people of Palestine as equivalent to apartheid in South Africa. He holds back from asserting that such Israeli conduct is racially motivated, but other writers in the alternative media have been less generous on that point.

Carter is meticulous in describing the stages and the failures of negotiation, and he provides the maps and documents that record each important stage. In so doing he makes clear that blaming the failures on Palestinians is a constant Israeli political game that is simply not supported by the facts. As a rule, the Israelis demand much and concede little or nothing, while the Palestinians are held, both by Israel and the United States, to an unreal standard of conduct, given that they are subject to constant repression by the Israelis.

The accuracy of that appraisal is well understood and documented by any serious observer of the Middle East situation. Palestine—Peace Not Apartheid provides a frank and, for a short book, comprehensive review of the issues, as well as a candid recital of the faults of the players. It does this through the eyes of the most constant insider/observer of the Middle East peace process. And it lays out the roles, the costs, and the consequences of American involvement. Because of its clarity, scope and candor, this book deserves the serious attention of all Americans. For better or worse, the United States is both part of the problem and vital to the solution.

Chapter 18.
Zionism and the Birth of Middle East Terrorism

2-9-07

Ilan Pappe's book, <u>The Ethnic Cleansing of Palestine</u>, is the most important work on the history of Palestine that has appeared in decades. Its central focus is the manner in which the Zionists designed and executed a plan to expel the Palestinian people from their homeland, to erase the history of those people from the landscape of the new state of Israel, and to create an ersatz history of the region to tell a false Israeli story. Pappe's history, told with integrity and clarity by a reputable, if sometimes controversial Israeli historian, provides an essential framework for understanding the birth and development of Middle East terrorism and insurgency. That may not have been Pappe's goal, but the inevitability of Palestinian insurgency emerges clearly from his account.

The first myth to die under Pappe's pen is Israeli innocence.

Terrell E Arnold

The Israeli version of Middle East turmoil has it that the entire fault lies with the Palestinians. While Lord Balfour's declaration may have been written with the good Lord's fingers crossed behind his back, the declaration actually specified that nothing was to be done to disturb the rights of the people already in Palestine. The declaration, realistic or not, expected that Jews who migrated to the region would somehow fit in the spaces between Palestinians.

However, there was no unoccupied space worth occupying. Rather, the Palestinians—close to a million of them—lived in more than a dozen towns and a thousand villages. Since the economy was traditional agriculture, each Palestinian village was the home and gathering place for villagers who farmed the surrounding near countryside. Since most human movements were on foot, the reality of community design was that the peasant farmers as well as their landlords created a new village cluster when distances exceeded the practical norms for daily foot travel between village and farmlands. Many of the villagers did not own the land they farmed; Palestinian landed gentry often owned it, but the villagers were wedded to the land as their principal if not sole livelihood.

Over centuries the size and shape of these communities had been well defined by the realities of traditional agriculture, that combination of land, water, climate, and lifestyle needed to sustain a given population. For centuries that combination was productive, but as the population slowly expanded there simply were no empty spaces. Here the Zionist design hit an insuperable barrier: There actually was no place for a Jewish national home in Palestine.

Initially the Zionist response to the space problem was to buy land from landowners who were often absentees. In traditional practice, the villagers working the land went with it when the land was sold, but that practice did not serve the purposes of the Zionists. Palestinians were pushed off the land the Zionists bought and Jewish immigrants replaced the Palestinians. Resistance to this intrusive pattern of displacement caused two Palestinian uprisings before World War II. The British suppressed both rebellions rather harshly and dispersed much of Palestinian leadership. However, perhaps surprisingly, no Palestinian insurgent group emerged from that experience.

The second myth the Zionists invented was that the Palestinians left voluntarily.

The problem, as Pappe defines it for the Zionists, was that leaving the Palestinians on the land did not allow creation of the Jewish national home either rapidly or expansively enough to meet their scheme. The newborn United Nations organization notionally set out to solve this problem right after World War II by partitioning Palestine. The UN neither consulted the Palestinians nor considered their interests. Rather its solution gave more than half of Palestine—in fact most of the best lands—to the new Jewish national home. However, the Palestinians still occupied all of it; Pappe estimates the Zionists had acquired less than 6% of the land at that stage. The UN scheme, innocently it seems, but certainly ill thought out, was that the Palestinians and the new Jewish settlers would live together.

That scheme simply did not fit Zionist plans. To reject it David Ben Gurion—eventual first Prime Minister, then de facto leader—conceived stage one of the ethnic cleansing of Palestine. Pappe says the operation was called plan D (for Dalat-a letter in the Aramaic alphabet). The ensuing process is what the Palestinian people call the Nakba or catastrophe of 1948. Ben Gurion and his core group took two Israeli terrorist groups, Stern and Irgun, as well as the young security force called Haganah and began to clear the land of Palestinians. During 1947 and 1948 these forces systematically murdered many Palestinian males and expelled the Palestinians from hundreds of villages and many from the traditional towns of Palestine except Jerusalem. They pushed more than 800,000 Palestinians into exile to Jordan—then including the West Bank—and surrounding countries.

Several massacres by Zionist terrorists, such as the killing of the people of the village of Deir Yassin near Jerusalem, received little to no international attention at the time (Albert Einstein and a small group of American Jewish notables wrote a letter about it to the New York Times, while Alfred Lilienthal's early 1950s book,

PALESTINE In Need of a Just God

<u>What Price Israel</u>, called sharp attention to it), but the great bulk of this Zionist war crime went virtually unnoticed in the United States and elsewhere in the west. Despite objections from knowledgeable officials in the State Department, the Truman administration, in power throughout the process, took no note of the crimes. Rather, in 1948 the United States was the first country to recognize the new state of Israel. That recognition essentially blessed the ethnic cleansing of Palestine.

Zionist myth number three says that Israel was founded in a barren wilderness that the Israelis made flower.

The Zionist PR scheme was to pretend they were putting deserving Jews into empty Palestinian lands. Pappe puts this myth to rest very persuasively. In a most literal sense, the Zionists buried the evidence. Systematically, as the Palestinian people were expelled their villages were destroyed. Buildings were pulled down and plowed under. In many cases fruit and olive trees, many centuries old, were kept but they were surrounded by new plantings including evergreens and other trees. Landmarks that were distinctively Palestinian were destroyed. The result was an "Israelized" landscape that, visitors were told, was the greening of the barren land that had existed before Jewish settlers transformed it. For people who knew little to nothing about the region or its history, meaning most Americans, the myth was persuasive at the time, and it pretty much remains so. But the myth can persist only if people ignore the fact

Terrell E Arnold

that more than four million Palestinians—the Nakba refugees, their children and grandchildren—today are crammed into the confining space of about 10% of their historic homeland, imprisoned by walls, razor wire and Israeli checkpoints in the least desirable parts of Palestine.

Myth number four is that the Israelis are the innocent victims of Palestinian terrorism.

This has to be the most carefully contrived and media protected fiction in history. For example, back last July the Israel Defense Force (IDF) invaded Lebanon. While the IDF was unable to find and decimate Hezbollah—the Shia insurgent group in southern Lebanon—as planned, Israeli aircraft conducted a virtual carpet bombing of the coastal regions of Lebanon, largely destroying the country's economic infrastructure. However, while the Lebanon campaign had the world's attention, the IDF undertook a similar attack on the Gaza Strip and West Bank open-air prisons of the Palestinians. That campaign of bombing, strafing, assassination and harassment of the Palestinian people has continued to the present. The Palestinians sporadically have fought back with rocket fire and suicide bombings, but the casualty count is brutally lopsided. Hundreds of Palestinians are killed or injured for every Israeli. The Israelis now have in prison more than 11,000 Palestinians, while the alleged cause celebre of the recent attacks is Palestinian confinement of one IDF soldier.

PALESTINE In Need of a Just God

Palestinian insurgency and terrorism are children of the Israeli pattern of repression.

The West Bank and the Gaza Strip, the areas where 90% of Palestinians are presently confined, have been under Israeli military occupation since 1967. The link between that condition and the evolution of Palestinian insurgent/ terrorist groups is absolutely clear.

Why is it that insurgent/terrorist group formation did not begin with the Nakba? The answer is inexact, but an article by the PLO representative to the United States, Afif Safieh, that appeared in the American Jewish paper FORWARD, suggests the explanation. By way of background, at the time of the Nakba many Palestinians appear to have believed that surrounding Arab countries would come to their rescue, and sporadic if weak military ventures by Egypt and others appear to have sustained this dream. The 1956 war that involved US, Britain and the Israelis should have demonstrated the hopelessness of that strategy, but the really decisive setbacks were Israeli capture of the West Bank in the 1967 war followed by the indecisive 1973 war. These failures persuaded Palestinians, as Safieh, put it, "that there was no military solution to the conflict" as well as no chance of a unitary Palestinian state in which Israelis and Palestinians could live together. As David Ignatius of the Washington Post noted in an August 2006 article, the 1973 war appeared to jolt all the players into recognizing that they had a stake in making peace.

Terrell E Arnold

That realization penetrated many different segments of the Palestinian people who were then variously dispersed in refugee camps in the West Bank, the Gaza Strip and surrounding countries. But, while moving toward negotiations, the Palestinians were not prepared to abandon paramilitary moves. According to Safieh, "the PLO aimed to remain a military factor so as to be accepted as a diplomatic actor."

The PLO, however, was not able to exert a singular control of Palestinian military impulses. Formed in 1964 in Egypt as a Palestinian nationalist umbrella group, the PLO has a history that reflects the ups and downs of the Middle East peace process. After Israel's successful 1967 war, the PLO became a breeding ground for militant groups. Initially Yasser Arafat brought his Fatah group into the PLO and the organization carried out numerous attacks against Israel and in the region. Dissatisfied with the PLO performance, the Abu Nidal organization (ANO) spun off from it and became the most aggressive Middle East terrorist organization. Reflecting extensive militant factionalism, other groups emerged, including the Popular Front for the Liberation of Palestine (PFLP) in 1967, the PFLP General Command in 1968, the Palestine Liberation Front in the mid 1970s, Palestine Islamic Jihaad in the mid 1970s, and various splinter groups of the above.

The most important groups formed in later years were Hamas in 1987 and the Al Aqsa Martyrs' Brigades in 2000. While Abu Nidal, Fatah, PFLP, and PFLP General Command carried out numerous attacks both within Palestine and Israel as well as regionally, the new arrivals, Hamas and Al Aqsa Brigades, confined their activities to Israel and Palestinian territory. With the death of Abu Nidal in 2002, that group appears to have curtailed its activities, and the recent pattern of Palestinian insurgent activity has been pretty much confined to Israel and the occupied territories of the West Bank and Gaza. A year before the 2006 Palestinian elections Hamas declared a unilateral ceasefire and concentrated on political action that resulted in Hamas winning a majority of the Assembly. That ceasefire still stands as Hamas policy, although there have been a few lapses by Hamas hardliners.

The peace process has moderated Palestinian terrorism patterns even as the Palestinians continued to lose ground.

Deciding in favor of the political process in 1974, Arafat pretty much held the PLO to a non-violent stance until the mid-1980s. That was partly responsive to the first Camp David round during Jimmy Carter's presidency. However, the prospect that those accords would actually go anywhere had pretty well dimmed by 1985. Nonetheless, the peace process received another boost via the signature of the so-called Oslo Accords by Yasser Arafat and Yitzhak Rabin in 1993. The Accords were actually signed in Washington, DC in a meeting hosted by Bill Clinton, and the better term for the document is

Terrell E Arnold

a Declaration of Principles on Interim Self Government Arrangements for Palestine.

While the Accords have been widely touted as a breakthrough and a binding set of principles for the parties, as Rabin pointed out in a letter to Arafat, the Declaration stated that "permanent status issues, such as Jerusalem, refugees, settlements, security arrangements and borders are to be excluded from the interim arrangements and that the outcome of the permanent status talks should not be prejudged or preempted by the interim arrangements."

Although this letter made clear that Israel had neither given anything away nor committed itself to doing so, Rabin was assassinated in November 1995. The gunman who did it said he was fearful that Rabin would give part of the holy land to the Palestinians. In effect, subsequent history has demonstrated that the assassin actually had nothing to fear; to date all Israeli leaders have successfully avoided giving away anything, except maybe the promised turnover of control over the Gaza Strip. The word "maybe" applies because even though Sharon executed a high-profile withdrawal from Gaza, the IDF still has the Strip locked down, regularly bombs it and rigorously controls traffic in or out.

Saudi Arabian King Abdullah's renewal of an Arab League peace proposal is the first significant move in several years.

PALESTINE In Need of a Just God

While early in the Bush administration the so-called Roadmap was proposed by the US, EU, UN and Russian Quartet, the most substantial feature of the map is a set of admonitions to the Palestinians as to what they must do to move toward negotiations. In any case, neither Ariel Sharon nor his successor Ehud Olmert signed on to the Roadmap, and so far the Israeli posture on King Abdullah's renewal of the Arab proposal is equally non-committal. Shimon Perez, the vice premier, said last week "the Saudi initiative...has merits." He summed it up cautiously by saying: "You come with your positions, and we will come with ours." That actually could represent a step forward, if the Israelis were to come to the table prepared to make real, here-now concessions on the final status issues that were supposed to have been settled—under the Oslo Accords—by negotiations no later than 1999. However, the Arab initiative calls for the Israelis to move back to the 1967 Green Line, as well as for resolution of the Palestinian refugee problem, in exchange for peace with the Arab world. Israeli refusal to talk about giving ground on such issues has effectively scuttled any prior peace initiative.

Compared to past proposals, the Arab initiative lands in a much different Palestinian milieu.

All previous negotiations have occurred with Yasser Arafat in the Palestinian lead and with his Fatah party politically in charge of the process. Since the January 2006 elections Hamas has had the political lead. Hamas leadership has proved exasperating to the US and Is-

Terrell E Arnold

rael because Prime Minister Ismail Haniyeh and other Hamas leaders have adopted the normal Israeli line: no concessions in advance. If Israeli leadership were to accept that even-handed concept, negotiations probably could begin tomorrow. For Israel to sit down for talks, however, it would have to start by accepting the fact that willingness to sit down on the other side of a negotiating table and do business with them is the only advance recognition Hamas seems prepared to extend.

If one reads Ilan Pappe's work carefully, the Zionist leadership of Israel is hung up firmly, perhaps terminally, on three issues: Any right of Palestinian return beyond the West Bank and Gaza, any concession of territory beyond the Gaza Strip and the slivers of Palestine now contained in the Bantustans where Palestinians are now confined, and any genuine concession of equality to the Palestinian people. The Zionist hope has been that their own resistance and unrelenting pressure from the United States would keep the 4 million Palestinians at bay until Israeli facts on the ground make any Palestinian state impossible. Then the Palestinians can either leave or remain in a slave status to the Israelis.

Hamas, it would appear, has forced the issue. Having refused to make any concessions, Hamas has reserved the right to apply as much force against Israel as Hamas resources can muster. The only thing holding that posture in check is the possibility, now dangled collectively by the Arabs together, that peace can be had for a simple price: Israel gets the part of Palestine it has confiscated so far, but only up to the 1967 green line; while the Palestinians get the rest of Palestine and some just settlement for their expulsion. Any simpler, more forgiving statement of the options is unlikely. Any hard line refusal of the Zionists to negotiate on the merits of those proposals is likely to assure renewal of older groups or the birth of new Palestinian groups to continue the struggle.

Chapter 19.
Palestine: An Honorable Solution

9-20-07

In the months since Hamas overcame Fatah efforts to destroy it in the Gaza Strip, the Middle East situation has moved toward a fragmented peace process revival. At least that is the picture painted by Mahmoud Abbas, Palestinian President and leader of Fatah. In creating that picture he has had the financial and political help of Israeli and US leadership, first to support Fatah's military effort to defeat Hamas in the Gaza Strip, and then, when that failed, to create a reduced Palestinian state in the West Bank that is dedicated to eliminating Hamas from the Palestinian political equation. However, eliminating Hamas will solve none of the real problems. That ultimately is up to Israel.

Hamas, in a sense, initiated the current crisis by winning a sizeable majority of the seats in the parliamentary elections of January 2006 in both the West Bank and the Gaza Strip. Empowered thereby to form a government, Hamas received little support and only truculent cooperation from President Abbas and Fatah.

Terrell E Arnold

Efforts of Arab governments, led by King Abdullah of Saudi Arabia, to implant a national unity government in Palestine were only nominally successful, because Fatah did not want to play. Moreover, Abbas and Fatah efforts to undermine Hamas, with strong US and Israeli support, made conflict inevitable. In the Gaza Strip, Hamas proved to be best organized, and drove Fatah from the scene. Hamas influence in the present West Bank remains significant but untested.

Abbas Creates His Own Government

Expelled from Gaza, President Abbas set out to form a new government by fiat. The Abbas solution, supported by both Israel and the US, was to form an exclusive West Bank government without Hamas and without an election. In effect, the US and Israel encouraged Abbas to violate the Palestinian constitution, behave as if the January 2006 election had not occurred, and form a new all-Fatah government for the West Bank. He was then encouraged to try to start peace talks with the Israelis, and to ignore Hamas and the 1.5 million Palestinians in the Gaza Strip.

In discussions so far between Abbas and Ehud Olmert, both have taken their standard positions: If he wants the support of the Palestinian people, Abbas has no choice but to move briskly into the critical issues. However, Olmert wants to continue the perennial Israeli tactic of deferring any discussion of real substance in favor of talking about atmospherics. For long time

PALESTINE In Need of a Just God

followers of the peace process, the situation has a tiresomely familiar look about it, but exclusion of a third of the Palestinians from the discussion is a radical departure from Palestinian history. Moreover, the climate has changed.

The Dark Emerging Israeli History

For starters, the history of Palestine and the growth of the State of Israel have become much clearer in recent accounts. Partly due to release of official Israeli government documents, but significantly due to the growing openness of commentary about the history of the region, the sordid truth of deliberate Israeli ethnic cleansing of the Palestinians beginning in 1947-48 is now widely available. By the mid1960s, Israeli forces (including the terrorist groups Stern and Irgun as well as the nascent Israel Defense Force called the Haganah) already had expelled the Palestinians from more than half of the country, and, Israeli and Arab legends to the contrary, up to that point Israeli forces had encountered no effective resistance.

Israel's quick and easy victory in the 1967 war demonstrated how limited future Arab resistance to Israeli takeover of Palestine was likely to be. As long as Israel remained under the US protective umbrella, military resistance was unlikely in any case. Before 1967, the Israelis had driven more than 800,000 Palestinians to UN refugee camps in the West Bank, the Gaza Strip and neighboring countries.

175

Terrell E Arnold

A number of recent works amply describe this history. Israeli historian Ilan Pappe's The Ethnic Cleansing of Palestine gives a clear picture of Israeli operations to expel the Palestinians, starting in 1947-48. Former President Jimmy Carter's Palestine-Peace Not Apartheid looks at the oppressive political results of the process. In their work, The Israel Lobby and US Foreign Policy, two American scholars, Stephen Walt and John Mearsheimer, explain, among other things, why Americans remain so ignorant or misinformed about it all.

In her recent book, The Roadmap to Nowhere, the late Professor Tanya Reinhart outlines the unholy alliance that has existed among the CIA, Israel's Mossad, and collaborating security forces of Fatah to eliminate Palestinian insurgent groups Hamas, Palestinian Islamic Jihad, and the Al Aqsa Brigades. As these sources make clear, since the Zionists started their takeover of Palestine, they have continually manipulated and repressed the Palestinians, all the while pretending to be part of a "peace process".

Early PLO Efforts Unsuccessful

When Arafat, with help from Abbas, formed the Palestine Liberation Organization in the 1960s, there appeared for the first time a possibility that the Palestinian people might have sufficient organization to negotiate with the Israelis. However, Arafat could not keep the Palestinians together. His own Fatah was then a terrorist group. But various original PLO subscribers such as

PALESTINE In Need of a Just God

Abu Nidal and Abu Ibrahim did not think that Arafat was militant enough and formed their own groups. What followed was the great wave of Middle East terrorism, the central driver of which was Palestinian dispossession by Israel. The existence of these groups, widely publicized in US law and policy, helped the Israelis to capture and keep the high ground of western opinion. Israel therefore encountered no real pressure to negotiate.

As Arafat withdrew his core organization from terrorism and moved the PLO into a more or less political mode, an opportunity for actual negotiations with the Israelis finally emerged. However, it soon became clear that the Israelis never had any interest in making a deal. At the time, and until the present, the Israelis have had the last word on the peace process. In the aftermath of failed negotiations that occurred at Camp David, Oslo, Camp David II and later, the Israelis insisted publicly that they had made reasonable peace overtures to the Palestinians, but the problem, the Israelis said, was that Arafat failed to respond. Mainstream media supported that posture in the United States, where the Palestinians had no effective spokesman. The truth was that the Israelis always temporized, never offered anything of substance, because they always put any discussion of the critical issues somewhere in the future.

Peace Efforts Went Nowhere

Arafat's inability to engage the Israelis in meaningful peace negotiations—more than matched by Israeli refusal to offer anything of substance—actually spawned the awkward notion in international media and political forums that Middle East peace was a "process". This essentially meant that, periodically driven by the US, Israeli and Palestinian representatives made repeated efforts to fire things up. However, those efforts contained no real substance as perceived by the Palestinians, while the Israelis pursued a long-term goal of avoiding any negotiation on Jerusalem, the right of return, and compensation for property the Israelis had confiscated.

Israel Grew As Palestine Shrank

Israel's Zionist leadership kept the substantive issues off the table, while they increased Israeli settlements in size and number. A support infrastructure of roads, walls, checkpoints, and "security" exclusion of Palestinians from such areas as the Jordan Valley steadily shrank the space open to Palestinians.

The following chart and sketch maps underscore the stages of takeover beginning before World War I and continuing to the present. As these data show, while the Palestinian, that is the non-Jewish population of the region, was more or less stable at around a million people through the early 1970s, the population grew rapidly thereafter, reaching over 4 million in 2000. That burgeoning population growth began with the rise of Middle East terrorism in the 1980s. In time, it generated the near panic of many Israelis regarding the "demo-

PALESTINE In Need of a Just God

graphic" crisis represented by a probability that, within Israel and the territories, Palestinians would outnumber Jews in a decade or so. As the Zionists and their supporters saw it, Israel's future as a Jewish state was in jeopardy.

Israel / Palestine: Arab / Jewish Population (1914-2000)

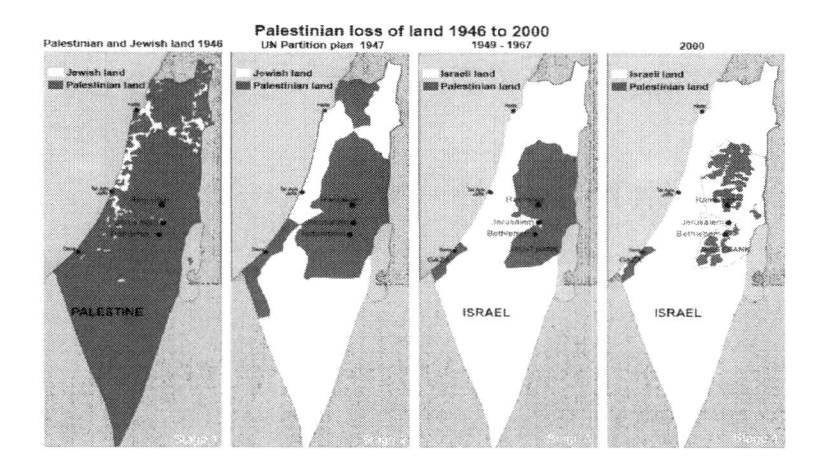

Palestinian loss of land 1946 to 2000

Palestinian and Jewish land 1946	UN Partition plan 1947	1949 - 1967	2000
Jewish land / Palestinian land	Jewish land / Palestinian land	Israeli land / Palestinian land	Israeli land / Palestinian land

As the sketch maps above indicate, by 1967 the Palestinians were crowded largely into the West Bank and the Gaza Strip. Since that time the crowding and competition of Israeli land uses have eaten away at space available to Palestinians. A picture ten years later than the 2000 snapshot would be even more fragmented.

Several Factors Drive Change

Rapid Palestinian population growth, along with Zionist political ambitions and the Israeli settlement movement thirst for space, drive the reluctance of Israeli leadership to engage in any negotiation with the Palestinians that might involve territorial concessions. The psychology of it is oppressive, as are the statistical results. The West Bank comprises a nominal 20% of Israel-Palestine land area. However, less than half of the West Bank actually is available to Palestinians.

The reality is that over 4.5 million Palestinians live in less than 10% of their ancient homeland. Moreover, the meandering wall, Israeli-only roads, and Palestinian "no-go" zones around settlements further reduce areas available to the Palestinians. In addition, that small area continues to shrink as Israeli settlements take more territory. What Palestinians have come to see is the probable total disappearance of their homeland in their lifetimes.

Hamas Enters the Scene

Hamas, the Islamic Resistance Movement, was born into this environment. The resulting landscape defined the political dynamics of the Movement. Sheikh Ahmed Yassin, who founded Hamas in 1987, pushed his organization as the most active insurgency against continued Israeli incursions. He did this at a time when Arafat was trying to keep the PLO and Fatah focused on political action and negotiations. High profile Hamas attacks against Israeli civil and military targets made Yassin a prime enemy of the Israelis. He was in and out of Israeli prisons for various attacks but refused to lower his profile. His elimination became a priority objective of the IDF, and in March 2004, a high profile Israeli helicopter attack assassinated him by firing missiles at his party as they left a mosque in the Gaza Strip. Yassin's death, and that of his successor, Abdul Azziz Rantizi, a month later, caused Hamas to change its leadership pattern, and it now has more than one publicly acknowledged leader.

Hamas leadership declared a unilateral ceasefire in 2005, and they kept that ceasefire in place until after heavy Israeli attacks on the Gaza Strip began in mid-2006. Meanwhile, Hamas used its time out of the terrorism front lines to enhance its political posture, to take care of its following in socio-economic terms, and to prepare candidates to run in the then upcoming elections of January 2006.

Hamas Transforms Itself

The Hamas victories in that election were landmark opportunities that Israel, the United States and much of the West chose to ignore. In less than two decades, a group formed by Ahmed Yassin as a hardcore domestic insurgent/ terrorist organization had moved itself nearly completely, certainly successfully, to the position of a political party. Hamas pulled off the transition that few modern terrorist groups have succeeded in making, and they did it essentially in one parliamentary election. However, while the Hamas parliamentary electoral landslide was declared by respected outside observers to be a free and fair election, the United States,

Terrell E Arnold

Israel, the European Union and much of the West, and, of course, Mahmoud Abbas and Fatah, rejected out of hand the fact that Hamas had become a successful political force in Palestine.

Hamas Agenda Popular With Many Palestinians

How Hamas had achieved that result was a case study in the correct way to retrieve communities from the warp of terrorism. Hamas initially achieved stature in Palestine because it stood for the right things as believed by Palestinians. It fought back against continuing Israeli encroachment on dwindling Palestinian living space. It frontally tackled the Israel Defense Force (IDF) with sufficient success for Hamas to become public enemy number one in the Israeli schematic. It articulated the correct posture toward Israel as many Palestinians saw it: Do not give up Jerusalem; insist on the right of return; insist on compensation for confiscated properties; and (the clanger in Israeli and outside opinion) refusal to recognize, in advance of serious negotiations, Israel's right to exist. Overall, Hamas stood closer to the Palestinian heart than any other group, including Fatah and the PLO. It was also doing an effective job of taking care of its following.

What the US, Israel, the UN and much of Europe have failed to take on board is the fact that Palestinians generally share the Hamas agenda. Abbas understands this well enough to insist on negotiating on the core issues from the first day. However, he and his outside supporters collectively fail to understand that Israel's right to exist is at best questionable in the mind of many Palestinians. Scarcely anyone in the region would consider the right a freebie to be given away voluntarily.

Israel Builds a State Without Honor

Israel has built its state by expelling the Palestinians, taking their lands without compensation, and killing or imprisoning them where they resisted. Despite the patently unlawful creation of the state, Palestinians and many other regional peoples may be prepared in the abstract to agree that the state exists. However, in their view, because of Israel's crimes, the state exists without legitimacy or honor.

Despite such criticism at home, and strong criticism in the United States by Alfred Lilienthal in his book, <u>What Price Israel</u>, the Israelis enjoyed virtual silence in the United States for over 50 years, and Israel simply has ignored the rights of the Palestinian people to build its state. The victims understandably consider the failure of the United States and the West to oppose that process as part of the crime.

An Honorable Solution Comes From Arab League

After Hamas took office it began to articulate—for anyone who was listening or reading carefully—a position that could eventually overcome the tragic flaw in the Israeli design by providing an honorable solution.

Terrell E Arnold

Hamas was very careful, even so, not to give anything away. Building on a proposal originally put forward by then Crown Prince Abdullah of Saudi Arabia at a Lebanon meeting of the Arab League in 2002, Hamas leaders said they were prepared to talk with Israel, but with everything on the table. That phrase, "everything on the table" meant that recognition of Israel, the well-known critical Palestinian issues, setting of defined borders, and such issues as permanent access between the Gaza Strip and the West Bank, would have to be subject to immediate discussion and decision. Hamas took an Israeli posture on this by stating they were not prepared to concede anything in advance.

Green Line Becomes Key to Israeli Honor

The "honorable" part of the Arab League proposal was Palestinian willingness to negotiate on a basis of Israeli withdrawal to the 1967 "green line". If Israel agreed to that outcome, even with minor variations, they could reach a permanent settlement with the Palestinians that would also be acceptable to the Arab League membership. To get the rest of the world, including the Palestinian people, to honor their historic land grab, all the Israelis have to do is (a) agree to stop at the Green Line, (b) meet the reasonable demands of the Palestinians respecting their rights, and (c) assure the Palestinians the freedom to have a future life in at least part of their ancestral homeland.

Hamas did not invent these choices. Selling them to the Palestinian people as a basis for permanent Middle East peace would be a remarkable achievement. Acceptance of them, or something very like them, is the only honorable two state solution available to the Israeli people. Israel's present path, confining the Palestinians behind walls in the shrinking spaces of the West Bank and Gaza, requires humankind at large to ignore Israeli creation of its much- cherished Jewish state simply by expelling or killing and confining the owners and taking their property. For the world to go on living with this requires ignoring a political sickness that plagued the last century and will plague this one ever more deeply.

Alternative Is A Single Democratic State

If Israel is not prepared to retreat to the green line, no Palestinian state is possible. Rather, as many expert observers, including the Israeli historian Ilan Pappe, and one-time Palestinian counsel John Whitbeck, have said, the solution is a single state founded on democratic principles. Even a leading Israeli peace activist, Uri Avnery of Gush Shalom, has argued that cannot happen, because it would mean an end to the idea of a Jewish state. However, in the long run that may be the only means to bring enduring peace to the Middle East.

Some Final Thoughts

As this article was being posted on rense.com, Israeli authorities announced all-out war against Hamas and the people in the Gaza Strip. That unilateral declaration, as the Israelis define it, gives them the right to turn off electric power and disrupt the flow of supplies to Gaza.

Terrell E Arnold

This is the most blatant attempt of Israel, so far, to break Palestinian resistance. As part of its campaign, already the Israelis have stopped at least a hundred nongovernmental organizations from continuing their humanitarian work in Gaza. Israeli authorities have even prohibited materials for school textbooks from entering Gaza. The formula seems to be that by keeping the Palestinians in the dark, hungry, unemployed, under assault, and ignorant, they eventually will accept their future choices: (a) leave, or (b) learn to live in an open-air prison.

The most disturbing aspect of this situation is the passive US, western, UN and many Islamic reactions to it. While the US has always said it preferred quiet diplomacy with the Israelis, that procedure obviously has had little effect on Israeli behavior. Some argue it has encouraged the Israelis to excess. While many of the world's Jews object to what is happening, pressure from within those communities has not deflected the Zionists from their chosen course.

A virtually prescient Israeli foresaw where this could lead nearly forty years ago. As Tanya Reinhart reports in her 2006 book, The Roadmap to Nowhere, the Israeli philosopher Yeshayahu Leibovitz made a harsh prediction that "Concentration camps would be erected by the Israeli rulers. Israel would be a state that would not deserve to exist." Significantly, Israel's perceived worst enemies, the Arab states, and Palestine's leading insurgents have offered an honorable solution.

Chapter 20.
The Ethnic Cleansing Of Palestine

10-28-07

Having sent up numerous trial balloons over the past several weeks, Israel now will work on shutting down the Gaza Strip. Having kept it virtually sealed off from the outside world ever since Hamas beat Fatah for control of it, Israel now plans to use creeping electric power outages to make life in that open-air prison totally intolerable. Since no major power appears to have objected loudly enough to the trial balloons, Israel seems confident it can shut Gaza down without significant political repercussions.

Gaza, indeed Palestine as a whole, now poses a unique case of global insensitivity, and we should ask why. Is it because everybody else considers the Palestinian people less than human? Is it because the Israelis still keep control of the moral high ground after six decades of unremitting ethnic cleansing? Is it because the killing and displacement of Palestinians has become so common a feature of the Middle East human scene that nobody cares? Is it because objections to the usually pointless lobbing of mortar shells across the Israeli boundary are so mind numbing that people stop looking at or listening to what is actually happening to the Palestinian people?

No. All of those probably figure in some degree in the mindless global reactions to the human tragedy that is Palestine, but the hammer is fear of the charge of anti-Semitism. In addition, the hammer most artfully pairs with the universal negative: "Terrorism." It simply does not matter what the Palestinians try to do in their own defense, so long as the Israelis and international media can lump any actions to fight back under the label "terrorism." Thus, the Israelis can surround Gaza with troops, barbed wire, checkpoints and a neighbor such as Egypt that, if anything, helps the Israelis; Israel's Defense Force can bomb and strafe Gaza targets indiscriminately; and because Gaza happens to be under the elected political leadership of a US—and Israeli—designated terrorist group, the outside world considers those actions all right.

The Zionists built the propaganda war around Palestine and promoted it through mainstream media, particularly American. The Zionists always have won it, no matter how repressively they deal with the Palestinians. Thus, humanity at large appears to have bought into the systematic theft of the Palestinian homeland by Zionists. It is therefore not surprising that, particularly in the Western view, even though the Israelis have taken all of Palestine up to the 1967 truce-line by force, the Palestinians simply should recognize Israel's right to the land and move on. People would treat no other scrap of land on the planet with such casual disregard for ownership.

Perhaps stranger still is the role Gaza plays in the run-up to pending Annapolis talks on a Middle East peace. It simply doesn't. The US host, Israel, and at least Fatah leader Abbas seem content with excluding a third of the Palestinian people from any role in the talks. That includes ignoring the Hamas supporters in the West Bank. However, the exclusion is more important than that. The US and Israeli players exclude Hamas and its supporters, in Gaza as well as the West Bank, because they stand for the only settlement that the Palestinian people—given any choice—would approve.

That choice, i.e. all of the West Bank and Gaza, with a capital in Jerusalem and a communications corridor, entails a colossal concession by the Palestinians: Acceptance, in perpetuity, of Israeli theft of their homeland. However, the way the Israelis and US promoters play the upcoming negotiations, the Palestinians have further major concessions to make, not least being acceptance of land trades to permit intrusive Israeli settlements in the West Bank, as well as concessions on the right of return and compensation for confiscated or destroyed property. Beyond that point, the Palestinians face hard trading on access to water, because at present they now get about 10% of the water per person that Israelis enjoy.

Terrell E Arnold

Because of such complications, most Middle East hands see dim prospects for the Annapolis talks. To be fair, Mahmoud Abbas seems fully aware of his inability to concede any of the main Palestinian demands. However, the Israeli delegation will insist on making no immediate concessions. Not only will the talks proceed without a full Palestinian delegation, it is simply unlikely that the Israelis will permit any substance to emerge from them. If that is the outcome, the gates will remain open to the steady Israeli encroachment on remaining Palestinian land until all of Palestine is absorbed into Israel.

The hang-up is that the Zionists can achieve the outcome they have so persistently sought only by driving the Palestinians out. Right now, because they simply refuse to give up, the Palestinians play into Zionist hands. Outsiders seem incapable of recognizing that, in similar circumstances, they would fight the Zionists tooth and nail. Thus, even if the Zionists have to lob the mortar shells over the fence into Israeli territory themselves, they will proceed to dismantle the remainder of Palestine without interference. Peace talks, such as they might be, will have value only as means to divert public attention from the final round of Israel's ethnic cleansing of all of Palestine.

Chapter 21.
Palestine—In Need of a Just God

6-7-08

Last week, a mobile billboard appeared on the streets of Washington, DC. That in itself was no novelty, but this billboard was designed for the first time to confront DC residents and politicians, to some degree the American public, with the Naqba. The word means catastrophe, and it refers to the beginning stage of Israel's ethnic cleansing of Palestine in 1947-48.

While Israelis and their supporters began a celebration on Washington's Mall of the sixtieth anniversary of the founding of Israel, the Naqba billboard was meant to face Americans with the cost of Israel's birth: The expulsion, including many killings, of nearly 800,000 Palestinians from their homes, farms, towns and villages. While the Palestinians fled to surrounding territories and neighboring countries of Jordan, Lebanon, Egypt, and Syria, the Israelis set about destroying the evidence of Palestinian culture, taking over and literally erasing towns and villages.

Terrell E Arnold

The Naqba catastrophe started in 1947—some say in the 19th century, but it never has ended. Slowly but inexorably the Palestinian people have been crowded into less and less of their historic homeland. Today they occupy maybe 5% of it, and the process goes on. New Israeli settlements spring up in Palestinian parts of Jerusalem, in Palestinian towns and farmlands, while more Palestinians are harassed, killed, wounded or imprisoned. Those who object in any way violently are treated as terrorists.

All of this happens in a world that often behaves insensitively to the plight of the Palestinians. Few people criticize; none interfere with Israeli operations. And the United States facilitates Israeli repression of the Palestinians by providing no-strings-attached grant aid of $3 billion a year along with even larger loans of military assistance funds. Those loans-which are routinely forgiven-are used by the Israelis to buy and sustain the modern weapons, aircraft, helicopters and bulldozers they employ to control the Palestinians while confiscating the tiny remainder of the Palestinian homeland. The largest share of America's economic aid goes to Israel, and well over half of the US economic aid budget goes to the combination of Israel, Egypt and Jordan. In addition, Israel is the largest US military aid recipient at upwards of $10 billion a year. Contrary to US law, but without effective US objection, Israel continues to use US military equipment to pursue its unrelenting takeover of Palestine from its people.

PALESTINE In Need of a Just God

It is worth remembering in this context that in the past sixty years only two American Presidents, both Republican, have put the screws to Israel for doing things they did not like. Eisenhower ordered the Treasury to put financial heat on the Government of Israel until they caved and got out of the Sinai and returned it to Egypt. Much later George Herbert Walker Bush roughed up Prime Minister Shamir in a set-to over loan guarantees. Compared to the damage that blind support for Israel has done to the US reputation and interests in the Middle East, those examples would appear to be small recompense.

To be fair, the United Nations has tried on numerous occasions to get governments to agree to condemn and restrain this Israeli campaign, and most governments have been receptive. However, the United States has always said no. Over the years the United States has vetoed over 40 UN Security Council resolutions that targeted Israeli misconduct. Various US officials have tried and continue to try what they call "quiet diplomacy" to persuade the Israelis to conform to international law and humanitarian practices. These entreaties, seldom if ever publicized, are invariably ignored, while US officials who persist often find their jobs terminated and/or their career prospects stunted.

Numerous commentators have noted the captive, at times openly slavish behavior of the United States where the subject is Israel. (During his May 2011 visit to Washington, Netanyahu rubbed that in with a vengeance to the repeated cliquish applause of the US Congress.) All list one or more reasons why that behavior is so strong. High in the roster are the so-called "Jewish vote" and access to Jewish sources of campaign financing. Since all major US presidential candidates find it necessary to make obeisance to Jewish community and Israeli leadership—as they have once again in 2008—those arguments seem compelling. As Barack Obama has discovered, competing candidates and their supporters do not hesitate to suggest that he is not a "strong enough supporter of Israel." This argument can and has been made to sound anti-Semitic.

As various Internet blog sites show, Obama has done considerable damage control around this allegation. However, one of his first speeches after winning the presidential nomination was to tell AIPAC (the American Israel Public Affairs Committee) how much he loves Israel.

On support for Israel, AIPAC lurks in the background, along with the Anti- Defamation League, ready to pounce on anyone who may be made to look non-supportive or anti-Semitic, or especially on any so-called "self-hating" Jew who objects to Israeli policies or conduct. Those ideas package nicely with a powerful AIPAC suggestion that any lack of support for Israel is anti-Semitic. The US Congress recently showed how captivated it is by such arguments when it voted almost unanimously for a resolution saluting Israeli statehood. Only one member bothered to mention Palestine's plight, and no member voted against the resolution.

There are holes in the case. There are dissenters both in Israel and in the United States. Among several Israeli groups, Peace Now is a large non-governmental group in Israel with a sizeable popular base. It works to achieve an independent Palestinian state within boundaries defined by Israel's 1967 borders. In the United States the landscape has been virtually unchallenged pro-Israel until quite recently. Now the unpretentiously named "J Street" group has emerged as a challenge to AIPAC and as an American pro-Israeli peace group that also works to help the Palestinians. The websites for both of these groups (peacenow.org and jstreet.org) are well worth studying.

Polls show that most American Jews vote on the basis of candidate positions on bread and butter issues, national security, welfare, and basic governance matters. In short they vote like most other Americans. Moreover, all American Jews do not vote for one candidate, although in eight out of the last nine presidential elections they voted overwhelmingly for Democratic candidates. The exception was 1980 when the vote was split pretty evenly between Democratic and Republican, which helped give the election to Ronald Reagan. Some observers suggest a similar Republican bunching of Jewish votes could occur in upcoming elections.

Terrell E Arnold

However, this is not merely about the Washington clout of Jewish voters or Israel lobbies. When George W. Bush met with Ariel Sharon at the White House in March 2001, he brought to the meeting a great deal more than support for Israel in the narrow Washington political sense. He had behind him the political backing of his Christian base.

That Christian base is not important as a beneficiary of Israeli/Jewish political clout or financial "largesse". It has played no significant role in the recent debate about the Israel lobby and the undue influence that lobby has on Washington political decisions. But parts of that base appear to have a direct spiritual, if not operational, alliance with the Zionists. That alliance is much less interested in the health of the State of Israel or its political clout among American politicians than it is in the preconditions for the End of Days. The driver of this alliance appears to be a basic religious deference to the Israelis because of their role in biblical prophecy. The net effect across much of Christendom is reluctance, if not outright refusal, to criticize Israeli policies and actions.

A genuinely perverse feature of this American Christian outlook is that it ignores the situation of a sizeable number of Palestinian Christians in the Holy Land. That number is said to be diminishing as many of them realize there is no future for them where they are. It is perverse indeed when the Holy Land itself has become unsafe for Christians. However, those who remain are subjected to either religious persecution or to treatment as a lower class of citizen. The approximate hierarchy seems to be: Ashkenazim are first class; Sephardim are second class, and non-Jews are yet a lower class.

There is no broad agreement in Christendom on the End of Days. But critical to those who believe strongly in the Book of Revelation and the prophecies of Daniel is a sequence of events that require that the Jews rebuild the temple that was destroyed by the Romans in 71CE. To do that, they have to be in charge of Jerusalem's Temple Mount. The two structures presently on the Mount are the ancient Islamic historic sites, Dome of the Rock and the Al Aqsa Mosque. There is considerable difference of opinion across the Christian world as to how important the temple is to the unfolding of the End of Days. However, the central argument is that the Antichrist who appears on the scene must stand in the temple, assert that he is God—a false god to be sure, and put an end to sacrifices that conventionally occurred in the historic temple and presumably would be occurring in the new one. The Antichrist obviously cannot fulfill this prophecy if the temple has not been rebuilt. Therefore, interest in rebuilding the temple is strong, at least in parts of Christendom, and efforts reportedly are being made to do so.

Efforts have gone so far as to establish that the original site of the temple can be used to rebuild at least the inner court-where the Antichrist must stand to assert his authority—without disturbing the Al Aqsa

Terrell E Arnold

Mosque or the sacred Dome of the Rock. Al Aqsa has standing in Islam behind only the Kaaba in Mecca and the mosque in Medina, the burial place of Mohammed. In religious terms, all of this is important because the End of Days is of equal importance in Christian, Jewish and Muslim religions, even though that fact is seldom mentioned in Christian discourse.

The prophecies of Daniel have given the Zionists a hold on American fundamentalist Christian loyalty that is blind to the humanitarian costs of Israeli treatment of the Palestinians or to the human costs of the End of Days scenario. To be fair, a number of denominations and faith-based associations, for example, the Presbyterians, as well as the National Council of Churches, have sought to distance themselves from Israel by such actions as persuading firms to stop doing business with Israeli organizations that take part in repression of the Palestinians. However, that campaign is hardly visible to most Americans. The core of Christian right support for the Bush administration appears to want no part of it. Bush apparently feels he can count on the Christian right commitment as he blindly supports the Israelis and ignores the Palestinians.

Most, if not all Palestinians are sons and daughters of Shem. In strict biblical terms therefore, they have equal rights to dignity and respect with any other person in Israel, greater Palestine, or, for that matter, anywhere on earth. But in the eyes of many Americans and Europeans, the Zionists have constructed the narrative

PALESTINE In Need of a Just God

of Middle East history cleverly to saddle the Palestinians with a collective guilt. Many Americans simply have bought the notion, cultivated by media, that the word "Palestinian" is a near synonym for "terrorist". Americans widely have also bought the assertion, central to the Zionist narrative, that every violent objection of any Palestinian to having his home invaded, his family members killed or imprisoned, or his entire tribe herded into an open air prison like Gaza is mere mindless terrorism.

Recent US official posturing has reinforced that image. Bush can justify current policy to his base because he has the Palestinians under Mahmoud Abbas cooperating with the Israelis. That means Palestinians in the West Bank are at least not actively interfering with preparations for the End of Days. Meanwhile, throughout the sketchy landscape of Palestinian territory in the West Bank, Israeli settlers are taking more land, slowly but surely eliminating the last vestiges of the Palestinian homeland.

On the other hand, Bush support for confinement of Hamas supporters and other Palestinians in Gaza can be presented as avoiding interference with long term plans for Israeli ownership and control of all of Palestine. That open air prison can remain full and its people desperate and many Americans will not care, so long as Gaza does not interfere with Israeli control of the Temple Mount or with work toward rebuilding the Temple.

Terrell E Arnold

There may be other ways to explain why the western world remains so blatantly insensitive to the needs of the Palestinian people. However, no conventional political argument makes any sense. Palestine is in desperate need of help, and that help simply is not forthcoming from civilized society. Feeding the hungry is a humanitarian act, and that mostly is occurring, but merely feeding people because they are the victims of deliberate confinement and punishment without doing anything to relieve their situation is a perverse and inhuman strategy.

The Palestinians surely are in need of a just God. Perhaps hard to believe, that is not the God around whom Christians contemplate the End of Days. As conceived by egocentric true believers, that God chose to honor the Christians by assumption, while punishing Jews by killing them if they did not convert to Christianity, and ignoring everybody else on the planet. In this formulation, the Palestinians are already largely ignored by the true believers who want the Temple Mount in Israeli hands at whatever cost to others who may actually have historic rights to the real estate. Those, in essence, are the Palestinians who don't count in this self-serving fundamentalist calculus. But then there are only about two billion Christians out of the world's nearly seven billion people. In principle, under the typical End of Days scenario, those non-Christian folk would simply not be considered in the assumption. If this is the scenario that actually plays itself out, a more just God is surely needed to see to the interests of most of mankind while the world destructs in cataclysmic Armageddon as fundamentalist Christians are lifted up to heaven.

The Zionists actually have calculated this scenario pretty carefully. Their hold on the loyalty of American fundamentalist Christians has more to do with immortality than with religion. By hewing faithfully to the importance of control over the Temple Mount, the Zionists have captivated the Christian right and, in principle, the Zionists can do no wrong so long as that control is assured. This imperative seems so compelling as to obliterate virtually every humanitarian consideration of the appalling human conditions created by Zionist repression of the Palestinians. In a perverse way, support of Israel by American politicians puts them on the side of the angels where the Christian right is concerned. Thus US Congressional actions that uncritically support Israel pass as good political judgment, while the shambles that is resultant American Middle East policy continues to mock long term American interests in the region.

It is vital to look directly at the results. American standing in the region has never been lower. Out of 500 million people in the region we can count on about 5 million (one percent!) as friends. Egypt and Jordan, who receive a third of total US economic assistance for their recognition of Israel, are allied with the US in the War on Terrorism because that helps them control their political opponents. America's much touted democratization program is actually frustrated by the War on

Terrell E Arnold

Terrorism, because that war allows virtually every oligarchic regime in the region to suppress its opposition groups by labeling them as terrorists.

Cooperating actively with Israel in bottling up Palestinians in the West Bank and confining those in Gaza in an open air prison makes the United States part of the problem, presently in no way part of the solution. In essence US leadership spends two-thirds to three-quarters of all US economic assistance to help Israel keep its control of the Palestinians from coming unglued. Ultimately we do much more to promote dissension and the accumulation of human grievances that lead to terrorism than we do to promote real American interests.

Fortunately for the Israelis, for other regional peoples, and for us, the Palestinians continue in overwhelming degree to suffer in silence. Primitive rockets into Sderot and other areas of the Negev desert, occasional body bombers and rock-throwing children are a surprisingly small human reaction to Israel's slow dispossession, murder and confinement of the Palestinians and constant harassment of them. To remind people of what is happening here, we are watching the slow and painful repression and dispossession of over 5 million Palestinians. Anywhere else on earth this would be genocide, and the political as well as practical consequences of it would be enormous.

In a world driven by rules of justice and equity, this simply would not be happening. Only the sheer arro-

PALESTINE In Need of a Just God

gance of power allows it. And only a political system as open as ours to blatant and corrupt orders of manipulation permits it to go on. Such orders of power and corruption nearly caused the end of human civilization on several occasions in our ancient history. Part of the problem in those days was the arrogance and corruption of the gods themselves. Christianity emerged from that experience as an escape from chaos by discovery and adherence to a just God. The Palestinians now need the services of that God more desperately than any other people on our planet.

Chapter 22.
Gaza's Tragic Link to the West's Terrorism Mindset

1-8-09

Last week the Israel Defense Force (IDF) started land operations aimed at destroying Hamas. So far, the IDF has killed over 700 Palestinians, wounded over 4,000 and indulged in reckless property destruction. The United States supplied the IDF with all the weapons and delivery system it needs to conduct this campaign. Meanwhile, US representatives in the UN have refused to go along with a UN Security Council motion to seek a ceasefire. Egypt and France are now leading an effort in Cairo to arrange a ceasefire, but the UN failure to act still holds. On a planet with daily more pressing needs for consensual behavior, one can reasonably ask: Why is this situation allowed to exist? As one of the original five members, the US, as well as China, Britain, France, and Russia, has veto power and can keep decisions of the Security Council from being enacted simply by refusing to go along with the common will.

Terrell E Arnold

When the UN was formed, the only way it could come into being, with the membership given, was to give any one of the big five veto power over all major decisions. That veto persists as an anachronism. While the Security Council has expanded to include ten newer members (none of whom has a veto), any one of those five can frustrate Council decision making. Since 1948 the United States has used that veto power more than forty times simply to prevent any UN decision to halt Israeli actions, to obtain redress from those actions, or to deal with on the ground consequences of Israeli moves in Palestine. Unless there is a rebellion in UN management the Israelis will be able to continue wreaking whatever havoc they have in mind while the so-called civilized world watches without interfering.

The US and Israel have a simple fixed perspective: Hamas is a terrorist group; it has not acquired any status by becoming a political party and winning a free election; anyone associated with it is a terrorist; any institutions created by Hamas or inherited by it to run Gaza are part of the terrorism network; there are no areas of Gaza that are exempt from attack. US/Israeli bottom line: Hamas must be destroyed and "collateral damage" is inevitable. The Congress of the United States is now engaged in passing a resolution that totally supports the Israeli actions in Gaza and lays the blame on Hamas

One may argue about the recent works of John Mearsheimer and Stephen Walt, Israeli historian Ilan Pappe, or former US President Jimmy Carter who describe the dark history of Israel's illegitimate growth or the strength and the moves of the Israel lobby. Underscoring that power, the congressional resolution now in process on the Hill showed up on the American Israel Public Affairs Committee (AIPAC) website before it was discussed in Congress. However, US use of its veto power in the UN tells the story of Israeli power over US policy better than any other single fact of post-World War II US history. That series of UN Security Council vetoes demonstrates the enormous Israeli Zionist influence over US Middle East policy of every American President since Harry Truman. President Truman, under enormous pro-Zionist lobby pressure at the time, made the US the first country to recognize the new state of Israel. For that Truman was roundly criticized by the British for supporting a basically rogue state.

President-elect Obama was quickly hooked into this tradition. Before he was even nominated, he went to a Washington meeting of AIPAC and swore he would give complete support to Israel. How that pledge will play in the current crisis will not become clear until after Obama is sworn in on January 20.

What does that have to do with the present crisis in Gaza? US use of its United Nations Security Council veto power has just cleared any major international obstruction from Israel's path of mayhem in Gaza. A prudent American would ask: How is this in the interest of the United States? Here is where the power of the Israel

Terrell E Arnold

lobby and the US preoccupation with terrorism come together.

A short history of modern terrorism will help. The decade of the 1970s was a freakish beginning, because much of the terrorist activity involved aircraft hijackings, often by Cubans. Those attacks were more of a nuisance than a national policy challenge. However, the takeover of US Embassy Tehran by Iranian revolutionaries on November 4, 1979 was a new wrinkle; in effect the Iranian revolutionary guard took those hostages to assure that the United States behaved itself while revolutionary leadership took control of Iran from America's close ally, the Shah of Iran. Except for an abortive attempt by Jimmy Carter to release our Iran hostages by force, the Iranian gambit succeeded. However, US official policy toward Iranian leadership is still fixated on that frustrating shift in the Middle East power equation.

From that point, Middle East terrorism began to dominate US foreign policy and much of its activity on the international scene. Several groups had grown and were growing around the eastern end of the Mediterranean. As indicated earlier, Palestine-related groups dominated this landscape: Abu Nidal, Yasser Arafat's Palestine Liberation Organization (the PLO) and its terrorist arm al Fatah, Hezbollah (the Party of God), the Lebanese Armed Revolutionary Faction, the Palestine Liberation Front, the Popular Front for the Liberation of Palestine (PFLP), the PFLP General Command, the PFLP Special Command, the Popular Struggle Front,

PALESTINE In Need of a Just God

Palestine Islamic Jihad, The Democratic Front for the Liberation of Palestine, 15 May, the al Aqsa Brigades, and Hamas all appeared and flowered pretty much in the 1970-1980s, and some into the 1990s. But note: these were groups spawned largely among Palestinians to pursue resolution of the grievances of the Palestinian people against the state of Israel. Their goal was to stop growth of the state of Israel at the expense of the Palestinian people.

Instead of focusing on why the eastern end of the Mediterranean suddenly had become such a rich terrorism generating environment, or what might be done about that, the US mainly reacted to the threat without examining its implications. The Israel lobby was already very busy touting that threat; the above-cited groups posed a threat to Israel; but as seen from the US, they were major threats to Americans. Lebanese groups posed major problems for the US in the early/mid 1980s by taking US hostages in Lebanon and blowing up the US Marine barracks in Beirut.

Beginning in that epoch, US policy froze around the subject of combating terrorism, meaning killing, confining or otherwise putting terrorist organizations out of business. Those became central goals of US policy. Rarely, if ever, were the questions asked: What exactly are the terrorists complaining about, which interest groups do they represent, what do they want, or what can we/other governments do about it? US antipathy to "terrorists" hardened in this period, and it has remained a central premise of US policy throughout the Bush administration War on Terrorism.

The PLO was founded by Arafat in the 1960s, and he developed Fatah as his arm to conduct terrorism against perceived enemies of the Palestinians. As a result of processes set in motion by the 1978 Camp David peace negotiations, Arafat, the PLO and Fatah were more or less brought in from the cold. They were recognized as the other side in a Middle East peace process that has gone through several unsuccessful gambits, but nonetheless remains a "process".

Efforts to advance the process in 2005 led to US-promoted elections in Palestine in early 2006. The goal may have been to reaffirm the leadership of the PLO and its post-Arafat leader, Mahmoud Abbas, but the result was a surprising electoral victory for Hamas candidates. The new government of Palestine was formed with Hamas in parliamentary leadership, but the US and Israel, along with Mahmoud Abbas and his party Fatah, wanted no part of it. While the US and Israel had accepted the gradual growth of the PLO and Fatah from terrorist organizations into political entities, both refused to recognize the political maturation and transition of Hamas. That has become an ironic US/Israeli blind spot.

In political arm wrestling with Hamas in 2007, designed to bring political control back under Fatah and the PLO, Abbas encouraged a Fatah campaign—including violence—that failed. Hamas was both more honest than the PLO and better organized for providing needed public services. It simply fought a successful battle for Palestinian hearts and minds by standing squarely for the things Palestinians want: peace, security, a right of return to their ancestral home, their own state with a capital in Jerusalem, and control of their lives. In the 2007 struggle for control of Gaza, Hamas was simply better organized and more widely supported than Fatah.

The US/Israeli response was to leave Hamas and Gaza to their own devices while forming an international alliance to boycott Hamas and frustrate its efforts to rule Gaza. Ironically, the West and Israel were boycotting the government of a territory that was occupied by the Israelis. The US and Israel focused on supporting Mahmoud Abbas and the PLO in the West Bank, essentially buying the support of West Bank Palestinians by providing resources to make them comfortable. That is the current situation in the West Bank. However, reactions by Palestinians in the West Bank to Israel's invasion of Gaza, in Israel itself, and in many overseas Palestinian communities show that Hamas has a great deal of support outside of Gaza.

The immediate US/Israeli goal is to make Hamas fail, both politically and as a terrorist organization. After months of pressure on Gaza, wrought by Israeli restrictions on people movements, prevention of shipments of foods, medicines and other goods needed to run an economy the size of a major American city, and day to

Terrell E Arnold

day harassment of the people, the US/Israeli strategy to unseat Hamas had failed.

Ironically, Israel has had it good with the support of US and other country aid. But it has used its air, land and sea power to deprive the people of Gaza of goods and services provided by foreign assistance that are essential to survival. In its effort to defeat Hamas, Israel simply ignored its responsibilities under international law for protecting an occupied population and it was not called to account for that. Rather, lacking UN intervention, and with support or acquiescence from the United States and others, Israel set out to starve the Gazans into submission.

For its part, Hamas demonstrated that it is capable of sustaining leadership in a progressively restricted, underfed and deprived situation, especially under pressures from a hostile outside world. Up to a few weeks ago, Hamas had used holes in fences, in some cases tunnels, into Egyptian territory to eke out meager supplies of necessities that regularly have been denied by Israeli forces that surround Gaza. However, possibly under threat of attack by Israel, or denial of assistance from the United States, or both, Egypt closed those frontier entries, and the squeeze tightened.

In spite of those ever increasing pressures, Hamas has not given up, and the people of Gaza have not rebelled against Hamas leadership. However, that demonstration aside, the US and Israel appear determined

PALESTINE In Need of a Just God

not to recognize the group's leadership, and to destroy Hamas and its following along with as many other Palestinians in Gaza as necessary to get that done. To date Hamas has exercised a moderate Islamic leadership. However, the US and Israel appear to have ignored the risks that mistreatment of an Islamic society would drive its members increasingly into conservatism and strict Islamic practices to protect itself.

Two blatant US and Israeli conveniences are at work here. First is the charge that Hamas is a "terrorist group". That charge actually resonates with current US policy in the War on Terrorism, but Hamas is the only known current insurgent group with responsibility for running a society. The "terrorist" label also now hangs from the second convenience for Israel: the continued lobbing of crude rockets into Israeli territory from inside Gaza by Hamas or other Palestinian insurgents such as the al Aqsa Brigades.

The Israeli public relations goal is to convince the outside world that its only concern is the firing of rockets by Palestinians into Israeli territory. However, that is a gigantic falsehood. The rockets mostly are harmless, directionless, of low power and yield, and there are few casualties. However, even such rockets can keep people in the area apprehensive, and their continual explosions are a political problem for actual and potential Israeli leaders who are facing a February election. As presented in western media, the rockets are the only excuse Israel has for the invasion.

Terrell E Arnold

In the months before the Israeli invasion of Gaza began, Palestinian rockets had killed one Israeli, while Israel Defense Force attacks had killed or wounded thousands of Palestinians. So far during the invasion Palestinian rockets reportedly have killed five Israelis; Israel Defense Force attackers have killed over 700 Palestinians and wounded over 4,000. Strangely, Israeli forces have been unable to stop the rockets, or maybe they allow the rockets to continue to justify their continued destruction of Gaza.

The Israeli story leaves out the true problem: Gaza is maintained by the Israel Defense Force as a large, open air prison. Ever since Sharon withdrew Israeli soldiers and settlers from Gaza in late 2005, the territory has been surrounded on three sides by Israeli military and marine forces, controlled from the air by Israeli military aircraft, and from the sea by Israeli naval forces. The people are constantly harassed and confined at all exit/entry points by Israel Defense Force guards and Israeli bureaucrats. The people of Gaza are selectively targeted for assassination, have thousands of relatives languishing without trial in Israeli prisons, and they are spied on and subverted relentlessly by a continuous flow of Mossad and other, including US, agents. The Palestinians are now trapped on Gaza's south side by refusal of the Egyptians to allow any traffic between Gaza and Egypt. The US/Israeli argument, largely underwritten by many members of the UN, is that any Palestinian who fights back against these conditions is a terrorist.

PALESTINE In Need of a Just God

Now the US seems bent on a repeat of the mistake it made during the Israeli invasion of Lebanon in 2006. When asked to support a UN sponsored effort to reach a ceasefire, the US refused for several days in order to give the Israel Defense Force time to put an end to Hezbollah. The IDF failed, but now the US is refusing once again to support a UN sponsored ceasefire in the hope, it would appear, that an Israeli ground invasion of Gaza will do what countless air attacks have failed to achieve: Put Hamas out of business.

Refusal to recognize the rights of the Palestinian people in Gaza and a narrow minded thirst for getting rid of Hamas (the so-called terrorist group) are driving the United States to support a totally inhumane approach to Gaza. The people of Gaza are being bloodied by Israel with US supplied weapons and logistics support. Israel's goal is to politically split Gaza off from Palestine while trashing the territory and its leadership. A growing number of Israelis and Jews throughout the world are appalled by the attack. A number predict the effort will fail. Some may even pray that will be the case, because if Gaza falls, the next round will be to dispose of the Palestinians in the West Bank.

The frustrating reality of this situation is that brute force is being used to persuade people that their best interests lie with becoming slaves. The US and Israel are not promising the people anything for giving up. Rather, the indicated future is that the Palestinians in Gaza, if they don't escape, will become the house-

Terrell E Arnold

broken captives that their West Bank counterparts have become. Israel is making no promises to any of them, and the United States is not pressing Israel for action on peace negotiations. Rather, with US help the Israelis are confining the Palestinians in an ever-shrinking piece of their homeland, meanwhile building settlements and destroying Palestinian homes. Each of those acts reduces that shrinking sliver of Palestine that used to be home.

The next step is for the Palestinians to be totally politically dispossessed. Whatever the Palestinian people are being told, the political goal driving Israel Defense Force attacks in Gaza is to eliminate any further Palestinian resistance to a choice between perpetual confinement or migration to some willing recipient country. The defining agency for Palestinian resistance is Hamas. Stopping the crude rockets into Sederot may please the residents of that region, but Tel Aviv is not really interested in that outcome. It knows that at most making and lobbing the rockets requires only a few people, and that can be restarted anytime, if provoked.

Hamas is a pain because it stands for the legitimate aspirations of the Palestinian people. Hamas therefore represents hope. And the last thing Israeli leadership wants is for Palestinians to believe they have a future in Palestine. That is really what the bloody invasion of Gaza is about.

PALESTINE In Need of a Just God

Is it truly in the United States interest to be associated with this agenda? President-elect Obama is in Washington now, and he obviously is being consulted about the resolution proceeding in Congress. That resolution, as of this writing, has passed in the Senate unanimously (lies, pretenses and exaggerations included) and will be put to a House vote January 9. If it passes, unless Obama rejects it now, he will be presumed to have agreed with it. If his support for this resolution emerges as ground truth, his administration will already have tied its hands in the Middle East. Did somebody say the US election was about change?

Chapter 23.
Hamas—A Political Portrait

9-30-10

Over the past few weeks, interviews conducted by the Jordanian newspaper Al Sabeel have painted the most complete picture that may exist in English on where Hamas stands on the leading Middle East issues. The interviews were conducted with Khaled Mesha'al who has chaired the Hamas Political Bureau for the past fifteen years. While Hamas is still labeled a terrorist organization by the United States, Israel and a few others, the interviews define a leadership and an organization of sophisticated political skills that is determined to use resistance for as long as needed to secure the political future of the Palestinian people. Where Middle Eastern developments may trend for either Hamas and the Palestinians or Israel may be obscure, but the picture of how Hamas thinks about the matter is clear-cut. It should be common knowledge for all who concern themselves in any way with the issues surrounding this conflict. What follows is a summary of Mesha'al's perspective with this writer's comments using heading key words borrowed from Al Sabeel, a Jordanian newspaper owned by the Muslim Brotherhood.

Terrell E Arnold

Negotiations

"Negotiating should not be a way of life", concludes Mesha'al, nor, in this author's view, is it merely an alternative to war. Rather, Mesha'al sees negotiation in a somewhat inverted version of the famous Clausewitz observation, "War is diplomacy by other means." The negotiating process is a tool for achieving the ends of war. In that state of mind, as Mesha'al sees it, you do not go to the negotiating table unless you have some power points to put on it. That means in essence you don't wait until you have lost your shirt to try to strike a deal. You aim to have enough power points to give you a decent shot at winning your objectives before you sit down. In these terms, he sees the basic prospects of the talks now underway as a likely donnybrook for the Palestinians. Thus, Mesha'al would refuse to participate, even if invited, which he has not been. He concludes that: "Exercised with great caution and under strict rules at the right time, it (negotiation) will be acceptable and useful in the context of conflict management; otherwise it will lead only to surrender and submission…"

Recognition

The Palestinians have been pressed hard to recognize Israel but so far have not done so, and Hamas, in particular, has taken much flak for its refusal to do so. In the Hamas view, as stated by Mesha'al, in this case recognition is not the simple act of accepting another state as is normal diplomatic practice between countries. Rather, Israel is asking the Palestinians to recognize the Zionist right to form a Jewish state (on land owned by

PALESTINE In Need of a Just God

the Palestinians) as well as to accept as legal what the Zionists have done to get there, including the occupation, countless murders, and the deliberate expulsion of about 800,000 people beginning in 1948. Both occupation and land theft are crimes, says Mesha'al, and neither should be blessed by recognition.

Pragmatic recognition

Simply admitting that Israel exists, in the Mesha'al view is equally flawed, because one has to accept the way the Zionists got there to say their state has a legal right to exist. The basic premise of this posture, according to Mesha'al, is that the Israelis need to clean up their act, stop stealing land, stop Judaizing Jerusalem, make amends for their numerous crimes in the process of creating Israel, and stop molesting the Palestinian people before Israel can even be approached in the legitimate diplomatic realm of recognition. Mesha'al rejects the idea of some that Israel deserves recognition basically as a trade for recognizing the PLO. However, he says the more critical matter is recognition of the Palestinian people and their rights, which Israel so far has refused to do.

Rejection of the Hamas Truce proposal

Hamas sees this problem through an optic of relative power. The first problem, says Mesha'al, is that their perceived superior power makes the US and Israel think they can impose any solution they want. Thus, they do not need to honor a truce proposal by people over whom they have overpowering advantage. In short, dealing with the Palestinians as equals is not in the cards. In any case, goes the Israeli/US argument, in time the Palestinians will settle...Some Arabs and Palestinians apparently have told the US and Israel: "Surround Hamas, financially and 'politically, and incite against them; do not open up to them directly, maintain your conditions and do not hurry. Hamas will ultimately succumb!" So far that has not worked, and the impression given by Mesha'al is that it is unlikely to work.

Hamas and the Jews

The perceptual trap for Hamas that would work in Israel and the west would be a charge, true or false, of anti-Semitism. Those who dream up this issue forget or did not notice the fact that, before the Zionist invasion, the Arabs, Christians, Jews, and non-sectarians lived in reasonable peace in Palestine. Mesha'al makes clear that Hamas fights the Zionists because they are occupiers and oppressors, not because they are Jews. In fact, the Ashkenazim Zionist ringleaders are not descended from Middle Eastern Jews but from central European Khazars. Still the Zionists regularly use the religious arguments to align people against the Palestinians and particularly against Hamas because it is Islamic.

International Relations

Mesh'al struggles a bit with the fact that up to now the Palestinians have lost many battles on the international relations front. This has been mainly due to the Israeli gambit (successful mainly in the United States) of posing itself as the innocent victim of Arab/Palestinian attacks and abuse, while it went innocently about creating the Jewish State in the allegedly empty spaces of Palestine. In the US particularly, and in Europe mostly, the picture of the Israelis as victims of Arab discrimination and terrorism was more or less a given until recently. The story of Zionist crime and theft of land was first told in some detail by Alfred Lilienthal in his book "What Price Israel" in 1953, but the scales did not really begin to fall off American and European eyes until early 2006 with publication of an article and a book by John Mearsheimer and Stephen Walt on The Israel Lobby and US Foreign Policy. Books immediately following that one, Israeli historian Ilan Pappe's "The Ethnic Cleansing of Palestine" and former President Jimmy Carter's "Peace Not Apartheid", painted a graphic picture of Israeli crimes against the Palestinians. However, Mesha'al and Hamas realized, perhaps later than they should have, that they were the victims of a well and diligently run propaganda campaign by Zionists and supporters. They began to fight back in international media, but they are still behind the curve.

So whither peace?

As the talks in Washington and Sharm el Sheikh, located at the foot of Egypt's Sinai Peninsula, have moved their slow length along, it has become increasingly evident that Mesha'al's reservations are, if anything, understating the difficulty and the hazards of the Palestinian position. Mahmoud Abbas, who, at least initially, refused to continue talks if the Netanyahu government refused to keep the let's pretend settlement freeze in place, appears to have been jockeyed into continuing talks even after the freeze has been lifted. At this time, there is no sign the fake freeze will be re-imposed. In short, with the Palestinians already in a weak—meaning no power cards on the table—position, the Israelis have added one more power card to their hand: With US acquiescence, the Zionists can and will continue rapidly to confiscate the best parts of what is left for any Palestinian state. They will do that with the politically powerful settler groups while the settlers' American financial backers look on with approval. Meanwhile, the Zionists and their supporters will hold their approval of President Obama's supporting role in this diplomatic charade as a US domestic political hammer over his head.

The best forecast for this situation is that the talks will go nowhere; therefore they will not formalize new wholesale losses of Palestinian position. The worst prospect is that the talks would yield a document that formalizes new Palestinian concessions, such as recognition of the Jewish state. For that the Israelis will pay the Palestinians nothing. Rather, the Israelis will buy this outcome by tossing campaign fund contributions into the party coffers of American politicians of all colorations. The contribution of American politicians, in turn, will be avidly subscribing to the continuing Israeli crime of stealing Palestine from its rightful owners.

Chapter 24.
The Hobson's Choice of Hamas

8-14-09

In late 2005 the Bush administration, along with the Israeli government of Ariel Sharon, promoted parliamentary elections in Palestine. The goal, obvious if unstated, was to provide a popular credential for the government that would be run by the expected to be victorious candidates, members of the Fatah party of Mahmoud Abbas. Since Abbas had won—against six other candidates—with a decisive 62% of the votes in a January 2005 election to succeed the late Yasser Arafat, the parliamentary election of January 2006 looked like a slam dunk. Hamas, participating for the first time in a national election, along with five or six small parties, stood against Fatah. The results, however, surprised most observers by giving the parliamentary majority to Hamas. Fatah won only 45 seats in the new parliament, while Hamas won an absolute majority of 74 in the 132 seat Palestinian People's Assembly.

Various pundits agonized over why this occurred. The conventional wisdom was that, after all, Hamas was nothing but a terrorist group. It had no political experience and ran no candidates of known political caliber on the Palestinian scene. As often happens with conventional wisdom, however, this explanation was wrong.

Since its formation in the aftermath of the Israeli invasion of Lebanon in 1982—some say it was adopted by Israel as a counter to Fatah—Hamas had been busy in the countryside. In both the West Bank and Gaza it had developed effective networks for community support. In a manner of speaking, Hamas emulated the performance of Hezbollah in Lebanon, effectively embedding itself in the towns and villages it served. By the election of 2006, Hamas had nearly two decades of community support experience under its belt. The people of those communities knew it well. They knew who unceasingly helped them, who had a well-deserved reputation for integrity, and who shared their thoughts on the future of Palestine. Rudely put, it was not Fatah.

At this point, outside forces designed the future evolution of Palestinian politics.

Palestine's government became a triumvirate. While Hamas was legally empowered to form a new government and did so, the United States and Israel refused to do business with it. Rather they encouraged other governments to ignore Hamas and they set about helping Abbas and Fatah to arrange a takeover, essentially a palace coup. Being better organized in its home base territory of Gaza, Hamas frustrated the 2007 Fatah takeover, retained power in a few pitched battles, while

PALESTINE In Need of a Just God

Abbas decided—with US and Israeli help—to take his remaining chips to the West Bank. Thus, the freely elected and street fight winner of an effort to rule Palestine was left to its own devices in Gaza.

In the West Bank, Abbas and Fatah were pretty well imprisoned by Israel and the United States. Abbas had a security force that was being enhanced—and effectively controlled—by a US general whose job ostensibly was training. The West Bank was surrounded, infiltrated and controlled by Israel Defense Force personnel who kept dissidents (especially Hamas members) in line, controlled all entry and exit points to and from the West Bank, and did not hesitate to shoot or confine anyone who looked possibly threatening. The name of this game was to keep the imprisoned dwellers in the open air prison of the West Bank moderately comfortable, but unable or disinclined to do anything about their circumstances.

The game plan for Gaza was radically different. Refusing to recognize the Hamas government, the US and Israel, with spotty help from others, set out to harass and starve the Gaza Strip into submission. In late 2008, it was clear that this plan was either working too slowly or not working at all. Hamas had continued to govern and find ways to avert starvation as the US/Israeli boycott of Gaza grew ever tighter. While some Fatah members had filtered out of the region to the West Bank, the people had not deserted Hamas.

Terrell E Arnold

American and Israeli assistance policies were used mercilessly to undermine Hamas and bring the people of Gaza to heel. All assisting governments were more or less successfully encouraged to avoid passing any assistance through Hamas. By late 2008 it was apparent that scarcity and near starvation tactics were working but too slowly, and more brutish measures were needed to get the already beleaguered people of the Gaza Strip in line. With the best and some of the latest US tools of military destruction freely supplied to them, the Israel Defense Force set out to destroy both Gaza and the will of its people. By the end of January 2009, Israel had virtually demolished Gaza with the IDF "Operation Cast Lead" invasion. An estimated 1,500 Palestinians had been killed and as many as 5,000 had been wounded. The rest of the world may have been appalled by Israeli brutality, but it chose not to condemn a major war crime.

The grim curtain that shields this atrocity is the charge of anti-Semitism. Under the rule set for this curtain, no one can criticize the murderous work of Israeli forces in Gaza without being called anti-Semitic. A major effort of Israel support groups in the US is now under way to pass so-called hate crime legislation that would make any criticism of Israel a crime under US law. Any Jewish person in the United States who might choose to oppose such a repressive law would be labeled a "self-hating Jew."

Finding a clear path through this political, spiritual, intellectual, and legal jungle is not easy for a Pales-

PALESTINE In Need of a Just God

tinian. It is excruciatingly difficult for a Palestinian politician who stands up in defense of the basic right of the Palestinian people to live and work freely in the country of their ancestry. Hamas does that more precisely and indeed more forcefully than any earlier Palestinian politicians. That is its political appeal.

In Israeli and US views up to this point, that has been the undoing of Hamas. The ostensible problem is that the charter of Hamas calls for the destruction of Israel. While such destruction might be acceptable in any other case as a way to get rid of an invading army that is followed by people who take without paying or giving, Israel has worked hard at keeping itself immune from such considerations.

Israel's approach is to use the war crime of the Holocaust to justify the war crime of the Naqba and sixty years of Palestinian repression. Jews who were not killed or confined found ways to leave Germany and the rest of Europe. Palestinians who were not killed or imprisoned in 1947-48 and following years have been driven out of most of Palestine. The Israelis portray this process as restitution. Clearer heads call this a war crime against Palestinians who had nothing to do with the crimes of Hitler's Germany. The Israeli crimes continue today as Israeli settlers grab more land (without paying for it) in the West Bank and the Israel Defense Force ejects Palestinians from their ancestral homes in Jerusalem. The shadow of the Holocaust blurs vision and mutes criticism.

Terrell E Arnold

The Palestinian problem is that people movements in historic Palestine are too generally interpreted as one-way. In the worst sense, Bush codified this pattern when in his September 2005 meeting with Sharon he referred to new Israeli settlements as "facts on the ground" that needed to be taken into account. That the land for settlements was taken forcefully from Palestinian owners without compensation did not enter the discussion. Sharon and his successors have seized on this concept with every new settlement. Currently, Netanyahu is accelerating new "facts on the ground" around East Jerusalem in order to foreclose any prospect of East Jerusalem as a future capital of a Palestinian state. What Palestinians would not give up by choice is thus taken from them by fiat.

The Hamas flaw—as defined by Israel and the US—is that it stands for halting and where possible reversing the Israeli takeover of Palestine. It has updated its agenda to the extent that it no longer expects to drive Israel into the sea. However, Hamas seeks (a) stopping the continuing takeover of Palestinian lands by settlers; (b) withdrawing Israelis back to the Green Line established at the end of the 1967 war—with perhaps some swaps to even out respective territories to Green Line equivalents, (c) recognition of the right of Palestinians to return; (d) compensation for those who are not allowed to return to their homes and farms; and (e) establishment of the Palestinian capital in East Jerusalem. This is basically the Palestinian aim as embodied in a 2002 Arab League proposal that is promoted currently by King Abdullah of Saudi Arabia.

PALESTINE In Need of a Just God

Recognizing that the Hamas position is close to the centerline of Palestinian thinking, Fatah held a conference in early August in which Mahmoud Abbas was confronted by an effort of Fatah members to recapture the Palestinian lead from Hamas. That involved the conferees taking a final position that moved close to the terms of the Arab League proposal. The problem with this position for Fatah is that the masters of Mahmoud Abbas are not the Palestinians, but the Israelis and Americans who reject the Hamas position. The US/Israeli position defines a Palestinian moderate as someone unwilling to fight back against Israel's continuing takeover of the country. Thus, anyone who would fight to keep significant and clearly defined parts of Palestine for its historic peoples is viewed as a "radical", or worse, a "terrorist". Hamas learned some time ago that fighting to preserve Palestine for the people of that historic territory was both bad for its reputation and harmful to its health. However, that Hamas idea resonated with most Palestinians. The US/Israeli goal, ever since the 2006 People's Assembly elections, has been to make the Palestinians pay for such bad political judgment.

The punishment has not worked. Most Palestinians still side with Hamas, as the Fatah conference demonstrated. What Fatah leadership saw was that the position led by Abbas since the 2006 election invites increasing political irrelevance. There is for the Palestinian people only one choice: Stick to their guns or watch their homeland evaporate into progressive Israeli settlements, while their much sought after capital gets turned into Israeli parks and condos for wealthy Israel supporters. Predicting the future is a risky undertaking, but the prospects are most likely that Hamas will not budge. After sixty years of repression, neither will the Palestinian people.

Chapter 25.
Linking Palestine to Iran

4-29-09

Israel appears to have decided, and the US seems unable to avoid the Israeli idea that (a) any solution to the six decade long Israeli takeover of Palestine from its people and (b) the as yet undemonstrated search by Iranian leadership for some nuclear weapons capability are inextricably linked. Even for ordinary mortals who are not steeped in the arcane Zionist strategies for avoiding peace this gambit may seem far-fetched, but just what actually is in it for the two leading parties, the United States and Israel?

Let's take Israel first. In February Israel had an election in which the political center of Israeli leadership, already teetering in that direction, moved decisively hard right. The newly selected Prime Minister, Benyamin Netanyahu, made it abundantly clear from his electioneering campaign to his first days in office that he has no intention to negotiate with the Palestinians. His Foreign Minister, Avigdor Lieberman, who is reputed to openly favor the assassination of Palestinians, rejected the US-sponsored Annapolis peace process of 2007. But Lieberman conveniently picked up on the US 2003 "Road Map" requirements as a reason to avoid any talks with the Palestinians. (The Map yet requires that the Palestinians cease and desist from any attacks on the Israelis—regardless of what the Israelis do—and recognize Israel's right to exist before any talks begin.)

The starting position of the new Obama administration on Middle East peace negotiations placed the newly elected Israeli leadership at risk of confrontation with the United States. Obama's first public decision on Middle East peace matters was to select former Senator George Mitchell as Special Envoy on the peace process. Mitchell's reputation for getting things done on Northern Ireland negotiations suggested he could mean business. Not only did this appointment suggest that Obama intended to stand back from the traditional lock-step US support for Israel; Mitchell could, in fact, become the honest broker that Middle East peace efforts have lacked virtually from the beginning.

Complicating the situation, as new Israeli leadership would see it, was the suggestion that Mitchell's agenda very likely would include talks with Hamas. Although it won probably the freest and fairest election (US-sponsored by the way) that has ever been held in the Middle East, Hamas is still treated as a terrorist group by the US and Israel. But charges of terrorism and Islamic affiliation aside, the real problem with Hamas, as Israeli leadership privately paint it, is that the group stands for the basic Palestinian agenda. Both the US and Israel have exaggerated the role that Iran plays in supporting Hamas, but neither to this point had suggested that the way to deal with Hamas was to have the Iranians do it.

Having indicated even before he was elected that he would talk with Iran, Obama told George Stephanopoulos on ABC in early January 2009 that "My belief is that engagement is the place to start." Without specifying that there might be preconditions, he did say that the US had "certain expectations". Among those expectations could be that Iran makes helpful efforts to rein in Hezbollah in Lebanon and Hamas in Palestine.

In that vein, Iranian President Ahmadinejad reportedly told ABC interviewers on April 26 that if the Palestinians and Israelis reached a two state solution, that would be "fine with us." In response to repeated, even hectoring questions, he made that point in several different ways, concluding that it is really up to the Palestinian people to decide. As if ignoring the obvious implications of Ahmadinejad's position, the US State Department spokesman, Robert Wood, said on Monday that the US wants Iran to rein in the groups it supports, meaning Hamas and Hezbollah, and "play a positive role in the region, which up until now it hasn't."

The implicit assumption of that remark is that the US is playing a positive role with two undeclared wars in the near vicinity, while watching passively as the Israelis

Terrell E Arnold

(1) continue to build settlements in the West Bank, (2) destroy Palestinian homes and businesses in East Jerusalem, (3) hold more than 9,000 Palestinians prisoner in Israeli hell holes without trial, and (4) confine the rest of the Palestinians to two open air prison camps in the West Bank and what is left of Gaza.

The "link-Palestine-with-Iran" gambit is multifaceted. By creating the foregoing kind of linkage, the US and Israel would make Iran a direct party to Middle East peace negotiations, assigning to Tehran responsibility for getting the Palestinians in line behind some peace plan. At no point up to now has direct Iranian involvement been a consideration. Moreover, with the leadership of Saudi King Abdullah, the Arab states collectively have put forward a peace proposition which Hamas has indicated it would accept, although Fatah has yet to speak up.

King Abdullah's proposal calls for "full Israeli withdrawal from all the Arab territories occupied since June 1967, in implementation of (United Nations) Security Council Resolutions 242 and 338, reaffirmed by the Madrid Conference of 1991 and the land-for-peace principle, and Israel's acceptance of an independent Palestinian state with East Jerusalem as its capital, in return for the establishment of normal relations in the context of a comprehensive peace with Israel". The Arab proposal does not recognize Israel as an all Jewish state. Since one-fifth of the population is presently Arab/Palestinian, such recognition would be contrary to fact. Note: The Iranians had no part in designing that proposal.

PALESTINE In Need of a Just God

The key question regarding this or any other peace proposal is whether the Israelis are ready to play. According to Israel's Deputy Foreign Minister, Danny Ayalon, Israeli readiness to deal on Palestine is firmly linked to Iran. As cited on April 24 in the Washington Post, he said "The new Israeli government will not move ahead on the core issues of peace talks with the Palestinians until it sees progress in US efforts to stop Iran's suspected pursuit of a nuclear weapon and limit Teheran's rising influence in the region." When Netanyahu meets in May with Obama, this issue will probably take center stage. This, in effect, will be pretty naked blackmail of the President.

Whatever else this Israeli position may suggest, it does not touch the bilateral issues between Israel and the Palestinian people. In truth, under present leadership, as both Netanyahu and Lieberman have indicated, the Israelis are not interested in negotiating. Herein lies the political elegance of passing the buck to the Iranians and to the Americans. It accomplishes two purposes. It says, for starters, that there is no need for Israeli negotiators to talk with the Palestinians until the Iranians get Hamas and Hezbollah in line, or, as Danny Ayalon suggests, parroting earlier remarks by Netanyahu, until the United States gets Iran in line. In these terms, the Netanyahu government would not have to take the heat for failing to start talks; it could say it is waiting either for Iran to do its job on Hamas and Hezbollah or for the United States to do its job on Iran.

Terrell E Arnold

The US benefit from this schematic is equally artful. Since the Israelis have no need to talk to the Palestinians until the Iran matters are off the table, the United States will not stand exposed if it defers any moves away from the Israelis. The Arab-Israel dispute does not actually need an honest broker until the Iranian work is done. All the hard domestic political maneuvering to distance the US from Israel is indefinitely deferrable, perhaps even until after the next presidential election—and the one after that.

Both the US and the Israelis must know that the basic premise of expecting Iran either to get Hamas and Hezbollah in line or to become a good regional citizen by American/Israeli definition is false. Iran may have leverage via financial and political/moral support, but the evidence is simply lacking that Iran controls the leadership, the membership, the roles, the agendas, or the acceptability of these two organizations in the communities where they reside. Both have morphed into successful political parties in their respective communities, and they both play public service roles that generate stronger loyalties than their political competitors. That is why Hamas won the Palestinian parliamentary election of 2006, and it is why Hezbollah has a third of the cabinet positions in Lebanon.

Iran might be able to convince both groups to cease and desist from attacks, but that could occur only in a situation where the Israelis are reliably known to have stood down. So long as the Israelis are attacking leaders or members of the groups, Iran could not be persuasive, and in any predictable absence of Israeli attacks, Iran is not needed to keep the peace.

On the broader issue raised by the Ayalon statement, Iran has interests in the region that comport with its size as one of the largest Middle Eastern countries, its energy exporter role as one of the world's major petroleum and natural gas sources, and its position as the leading country in Shia Islam—to say nothing of its long cultural history. The notion that those attributes can easily be suppressed in line with Israeli and US preferences is simply naïve.

The inescapable bottom line here is that the Zionists are blackmailing the Obama administration. Judging that Obama feels politically compelled to make visible progress on Palestine peace negotiations, the Zionists are using the opportunity to trade on Obama's necessity. The Israelis already have parlayed a something for nothing strategy into the ethnic cleansing of most of Palestine—without paying any of the people expelled. Now Israeli leadership can see in the Iran gambit a grand opportunity to get more for nothing. They propose to trade future movement that in their own interest they should make on Palestine for forceful US action against Iran. That might be a great Israeli windfall, but it assuredly could cost the United States and the Iranians dearly.

Terrell E Arnold

As usual, the Palestinians will pay no matter how this goes. Life may be somewhat better in the West Bank, but it is harsh in Gaza. And there is no evident pressure on the Israelis to improve that situation. Rather, the US and Israel, with European acquiescence, continue to deny assistance by refusing to allow the elected government, Hamas, to handle aid supplies in Gaza or elsewhere. The longer this stretches out the more misery accrues to already miserable people. A grand US-Israeli strategy to entrap Iran will progress, if at all, at the expense of the people of Palestine.

As experts have reminded us numerous times in the past several decades, the long term ideal would be a nuclear weapons-free Middle East. However, the Israelis are unlikely to buy that, preferring instead to bolster their monopoly. As the next best choice, there has to be an honest effort by the leading nations of the Nuclear Non-Proliferation Treaty to keep Iran comfortable with nuclear power generation levels of energy materials processing. That would be infinitely more likely to prosper than past attempts to suppress Iranian rights under the treaty. And the best that can be hoped for on that path is an outcome that leaves for some future date any Iranian decision about weaponry. Continuing Israeli threats, bolstered by American displays of force, will simply cause the Iranians, in prudence, to make that decision sooner rather than later. Herein lies the most dangerous Palestine-Iran linkage problem, but once the realistic choices are faced, it is the easiest to resolve.

Chapter 26.
Jerusalem: Historical Disaster in the Making

8-10-09

Benyamin Netanyahu has launched an Israeli effort to achieve the earliest possible end to any Palestinian dreams about statehood. Ignoring US White House and other international pressures to cease and desist, settlers are expanding their grip on the most choice lands—and waters—of the West Bank. Meanwhile, an official Israeli scramble is on to foreclose any prospects of a Palestinian capital in East Jerusalem.

The assaults (some long standing), include refusal to allow Palestinians to enter East Jerusalem, confiscation of property for "state" uses, condemnation and destruction of "illegally built" Palestinian homes, refusal of building permits to Palestinians, and continual harassment of those who refuse to leave. Tearing down the old Shepherd Hotel and building apartments for Jews in its place, and giving Jews permission to live anywhere, are just the latest steps in the gross Israeli process of expelling Palestinians from Jerusalem.

Election of a new American President, Barack Obama, with an agenda to bring peace to Palestine appears to have put the cat among Zionism's pigeons. To see where this is going requires a bit of history. In 1947-48, when the Zionist ethnic cleansing of Palestine began under Prime Minister-to-be David Ben-Gurion, the Israeli forces adopted a basic program design that has persisted to the present. As Israeli terrorist groups, Stern and Irgun, began destroying Palestinian homes, farms and villages, the goal was to destroy the evidence of Palestinian occupancy, erase the history and create a Zionist narrative in its place. That narrative, as touted in the West, became: The Israeli people took their ancient home, which had become an unoccupied and undeveloped land and turned it into a thriving new society.

People who had never been to or perhaps never even seen pictures of Palestine bought into this narrative. It worked especially well on people who were ignorant of the Middle East. It has worked well with fundamentalist American and other Christians dedicated to preparation for the biblically prophesied "end of days." Scripturally at least, that event requires Jewish control of Jerusalem's Temple Mount and reconstruction of the temple that was destroyed by the Romans in 71 CE.

The immediate Zionist quandary is what to do about Jerusalem. Jerusalem has a history, some of it

PALESTINE In Need of a Just God

pretty spotty, of more than three millennia. Biblically that goes back to a period when Moses led the Children of Israel out of Egypt, across the Sinai desert and to Judea. Without repeating that story, the period relevant to modern times is the period of King Solomon, the son of King David, who built the first temple on what is now the Temple Mount of Old Jerusalem. (Realistically, Solomon's foundation stones would be the base for a new temple.) Since the birth of Christ and the founding of Christianity, followed by the birth of Mohammed and the founding of Islam, Old Jerusalem has been a sacred city to all three Abrahamic religions: Judaism, Christianity and Islam.

The hard right Zionist leadership of Israel, led by Benyamin Netanyahu, wants Jerusalem to become the exclusive capital of an all Jewish state of Israel. Since founding their state in 1948, the Israelis have sought to make Jerusalem their capital. Jews have been a minor population of the region and the city for virtually all of the past two thousand years, but as Abraham told it, God promised the land of Israel to his descendants. Except for this promise recorded in the sacred writings of both Jews and Christians, the Israelis have no claim on the lands of Palestine. The validity of the claim is even less real today, since the core population of the Zionists is Central European converts to Judaism, not the legendary "people of the book" (called that because they were referred to in holy scriptures) for whom and to whom the promise is said to have been made.

Terrell E Arnold

Aside from dubious rights of ownership, an equally large and intractable expulsion problem hovers above the city like a dark religious cape: the future of the historic Temple Mount. According to various scholarly estimates, Solomon built the first temple on the mount in about 950 BCE (Before the Common Era). His temple, conceived by King David as the repository for the Ark of the Covenant, was a sprawling structure of more than 16,000 square feet with a ceiling 50 feet high. The main foundation stones, brought by unknown means from quarries miles away, are each estimated to weigh more than 20 tons. Even though Solomon's temple was apparently razed to the ground in 586 BCE by the Babylonians, those foundation stones were used to build a second temple sometime in the 600 years before 71 CE. In that year the temple was destroyed again, this time by the Romans. The foundation stones of Solomon's temple are still in place, capping the Temple Mount.

Complicating Jewish and Christian use of the Mount for new construction purposes are two Islamic monuments: The Dome of the Rock, finished around 691 CE, and the Al Aqsa Mosque. The mosque has a history longer than the Dome of the Rock. It is considered the second oldest mosque in Islam (after Mecca), and references to it antedate Mohammed's own construction of the mosque at Medina in 622 CE. Al Aqsa was destroyed or damaged and rebuilt about five times. The present Al Aqsa, completed about 1035 CE, is considered the third most important site in Islam, Muslims believe that Mohammed, whether in the flesh or in spirit, was transported from Mecca to Jerusalem's Temple Mount in one night, and that event made Jerusalem Islam's third holiest of places. That flight was the reason why in the early days of Islam Muslims prayed facing the Temple Mount in Jerusalem rather than the Kaaba in Mecca. That change in Islamic practice occurred about a year and a half after the migration of Mohammed and his followers to Medina from Mecca, the event known as the Hijra (Hegira in Latin) that occurred in about mid 622 CE.

The real point of this history, as many religious, historical and regional scholars point out, is that the Temple Mount is a sacred site in "all three" Abrahamic religions. However, Israel captured the whole of Jerusalem when it took the West Bank from Jordan in the 1967 war. At that time Israel turned Muslim holy places over to an Islamic authority called in Arabic the Waqf. The term means inalienable religious endowment. Since 1967, the Waqf has prevented Jews or others from entering or performing religious ceremonies on the Mount. Israelis, notably those in the Temple Movement and orthodox Jews, have pressed Israeli authorities to override those restrictions, and it appears that the Netanyahu government intends to follow through, perhaps opening the Mount to followers of all three religions.

So long as visitors do nothing to invade or desecrate the Dome of the Rock or the Al Aqsa Mosque, it would seem there is no honest choice but to open the Mount. If properly approached, rather than arbitrarily confronted, one can hope the Waqf, along with Muslims in general, would see the light on this.

However, Israeli groups have not been standing still. A recent edition of the Egyptian weekly Al Ahram reported that "three huge granite stones rest comfortably on the top of Midbar Sinai Street....in Jerusalem's northernmost district. Cut to specification, the imposing stones represent one of several preparations by the Temple Mount and Land of Israel Faithful Movement to erect a Third Temple on the Haram Al-Sharaf Temple Mount." That is the Arabic name for the Noble Sanctuary that includes the Dome of the Rock, the Al Aqsa Mosque and their surrounding gardens. Al Ahram is right in suggesting that the stones in waiting are a provocation, one that the Israeli government has done nothing to halt. Rather, Al Ahram speculates "Neglect and passivity have led to a belief by Israeli leadership that an eventual Muslim reaction to the increasing provocations will give the Israel Defense Force an excuse to seize total control of the Holy Basin." The term, Holy Basin, is used by numerous people to mean the Temple Mount, Mount Zion, various Christian holy sites and the Mount of Olives. It is the spiritual heart of Old Jerusalem for Christians, Jews and Muslims.

This is the historical footprint of Christianity. For that reason, one of the first acts of the then newly formed United Nations in 1947 was to propose holding Jerusalem as a UN administered territory. President Bill Clinton proposed to administer the Holy Basin under a "special regime". It is a critical part of the territory of East Jerusalem that Netanyahu may try to incorporate into a greater Jerusalem in his effort to expunge the Palestinians from Jerusalem and make it the exclusive capital of Israel. As various reports out of Jerusalem indicate, the Netanyahu/Zionist schematic is not merely to take exclusive control of Old Jerusalem including the Temple Mount, but to erase all evidence of history in the area except for limited and scattered Jewish sites and artifacts. In that direction, the Israelis already have destroyed one Old Jerusalem Palestinian area including its mosque. In one zone of the old city, the Israeli scheme is to destroy Palestinian homes and businesses and turn the area into a park.

Meanwhile, street names and local place names are being reissued in Hebrew versions that erase the evidences of the non-Jewish past. To recreate Old Jerusalem around its remnants of the Jewish past, there are major symbolic hurdles: Important ones are the Dome of the Rock and Al Aqsa Mosque. However, there are many more Christians than Muslim sites. Among the most widely cherished by Christian denominations being the Church of the Holy Sepulchre (built around 326 CE), the Garden Tomb, the Church of St. John, the Condemnation Chapel, the Flagellation Chapel, and Mary's Tomb.

Many Israelis, especially among the young it seems, would not take to an allegedly exclusive Israeli capital with a landscape dominated by historic Muslim and

Terrell E Arnold

Christian monuments. As that history makes clear, redesigning East Jerusalem to focus on its limited Jewish past has power to offend more than half of humanity, counting only the Christian and Muslim peoples. So far, however, the most visible offenses have been directed against Muslims and their communities. As events move in that direction, a major crisis is brewing in the whole of Islam. Over a billion Muslims hold the holy places on the Temple Mount as the third most holy of their roster of sacred precincts. If Israeli authorities actually try to break the Waqf control of the Mount or to take it away, and especially if any harm is done to the Dome of the Rock or Al Aqsa Mosque, street war will break out.

Archaeologists and scholars who have tried to open historic tunnels or rooms below the Mount have excited demonstrations, bombings, and other outbursts. Those will prove to have been tame by comparison with the probable Islamic reactions to perceived desecration of the Mount by starting to build something new on it. Such reactions are certain if any new temple construction (as one group proposes) would cause damage to the Dome of the Rock or require its destruction. Israel may well use such outbursts to take over the Mount by warlike means and no doubt will succeed on the ground. It will not be able to control reactions, however, that will erupt throughout the region.

No doubt the time is approaching when the Temple Mount must become the commonly accessible property of all three Abrahamic faiths. However, the future of the

PALESTINE In Need of a Just God

Temple Mount simply cannot be decided by a military strike. If there is any change, it should be determined by appropriate representatives of all three religious communities. Practically speaking, the lead has to be taken by the Waqf. The Israeli goal, however, as being pursued by Netanyahu, is to incorporate East Jerusalem, indeed all areas of the ancient city of Jerusalem, in a singular capital for Greater Israel. The Israelis want a world class capital, however, and at least some believe that will not work if the principal ancient sites, place names and relics pertain mainly to Islamic and Christian history.

Here the egoistic Israeli narrative comes into play. From the beginning of Israeli ethnic cleansing of Palestine, as the Israelis conquered territory they destroyed farms and villages and replaced them with their own farms, homes, forests, whatever to fit the story that Israelis took the barren wasteland of Palestine and turned it into a modern state.

That narrative is now being played out in a new dimension in East Jerusalem as the Israelis destroy Palestinian homes, streets, neighborhoods, and historic sites in the old city. The design of Greater Israel, ruthlessly pursued in the whole of ancient Palestine so far occupied by the Israelis, has been to obliterate signs of Palestinian presence. It is the invention of a new archaeology that preserves only the limited signs of an historic Jewish presence. This is not a mere verbal rewriting of history, but a systematic deletion of the evidences of the past.

Terrell E Arnold

The Israeli approach to a takeover, indeed makeover, of Old Jerusalem is both elaborate and extravagant. Construction of new Jewish homes on the sites of destroyed Palestinian homes progresses rapidly. On one eleven acre site a gated community of million-dollar condominium residences is being offered to wealthy US investors.

Meanwhile, a schizophrenic pattern of US policy is being presented to the Israelis. The recent visit of 25 members of Congress under the leadership of House Republican Whip Eric Cantor illustrates the extremes. Contrary to official US policy, that delegation sided unanimously with Netanyahu on continuing settlement construction, while Cantor drove the point home by visiting a settlement that was clearly in West Bank Palestinian territory and that the Israel Supreme court had declared illegal. Cantor further revealed the extremes of Washington political thinking when he pooh-poohed the idea of the 1967 Green Line as the border between Israel and the Palestinian state and he criticized the White House for taking exception to Israeli expulsion of two Palestinian families from their East Jerusalem homes. Cantor thus illustrates, where Israel is concerned, a dangerous tendency of many high ranking American politicians to sound suddenly as if they work for a foreign government, Israel, not the US for which they were elected.

The reality that Congress, the Obama administration and the American public must now take on board

PALESTINE In Need of a Just God

is that the situation is reaching dangerous, more than likely explosive, intensity. The Israeli right obviously anticipates that it can act in ways that result in an Islamic explosion and get the whole problem blamed on the Palestinians. The Israeli actions further perfect a strategy that has worked for at least six decades: Keep most Americans ignorant of real life at the eastern end of the Mediterranean, keep taking Palestine away from its historic owners, and continue to play the victim of Palestinian "terrorism". The strategy may decline in value as more and more people become aware of the Palestine situation. However, the danger is that, as repeatedly in the past, the Israelis will create new "facts on the ground", count on the United States to defend its right to do so, and stall out genuine peace talks. Under this strategy the Palestinian people—- immediately those of East Jerusalem—- will go on paying the price for Israel's continued ethnic cleansing of Palestine.

Chapter 27.
Palestine and the Demise of Conscience

9-10-09

For nearly a century the Palestinian people have felt the pressures of outsiders scheming to take over their homeland. For the past sixty years the invaders have systematically undertaken the ethnic cleansing of Palestine to make way for new Israelis. For this purpose the invaders have constructed a narrative the central theme of which is summarized as follows: God gave this land to us five or six thousand years ago, and the fact that we have seldom lived here in that period is immaterial. No matter who has lived on the land for the past several thousand years, it is ours and we intend to take it. We do not intend to pay for the land or the property on it that we may destroy, and we do not intend to tolerate the future presence of any historic owner on this land. We, the founders and ringleaders of this scheme, the Ashkenazim, do not have ancestors who were ever a part of this land, but we will take this land anyway and found a Jewish state.

In line with this story, since 1947-48 the true believers in this Ashkenazim scheme have driven hundreds of thousands of Palestinians from their farms, homes and businesses; they have killed and imprisoned thousands more; and they currently keep 4 plus million survivors and their offspring in two open air prisons—the Gaza Strip and shrinking portions of the region known as the West Bank of the Jordan River. The followers of this Ashkenazim scheme barely tolerate the presence of more than 1.25 million descendants of the original Palestinian inhabitants of the land in Israel. Meanwhile, the subscribers to a scheme called Eretz Yisrael, or Greater Israel, work toward the eventual expulsion of all non-Jews from the territory that the Old Testament of Christendom, also known as the Torah of Judaism, says God promised to Abraham and his descendants.

Meanwhile, in a seemingly perverse treatment of the Zionist scheme that the Ashkenazim and their followers pursue, God and nature take care of their own. The reality is that the nominally Jewish (at least by religious affiliation) and the nominally Arab (meaning non-Jewish) peoples of the region are about equal in number. In the nature of things, however, the Arabs, threatened on all sides by poverty, confinement, expulsion or extinction, have a relatively high birthrate. The Ashkenazim and their followers, nominally including the indigenous Palestinian Jews, are more comfortable, less threatened and less fertile. In fairly short order, barring a catastrophe, the Palestinians will outnumber the Jews. That is the nearby reality facing the Zionists. As noted in the opening chapter of this book, a Jewish state with a majority of Palestinians is simply not thinkable.

PALESTINE In Need of a Just God

But a Jewish state that ignores the rights of the Palestinians should also be unthinkable. The Goldstone Report just released by the UN Commission on Human Rights rightly and clearly condemns Israeli excesses in the war on Gaza. However, in a strained effort to be even-handed, the Commission also condemns Palestinian lobbing of rockets into Israeli territory while it was being bombed daily by (US-built) Israeli aircraft. The report does not question Israel's right to attack Gaza, only its excesses in doing so, but it does not concede any Hamas right to attack adjacent areas of Israel. The report also bemoans the continued imprisonment of one Israeli soldier, Gilad Shilat, while failing to mention the 9,000 or more Palestinians in Israeli prisons. A fair comparison of Israeli actions in Gaza would put Israel's military operation against Gaza—Cast Lead—on one side and a few Palestinian pebbles on the other, but Goldstone himself, a highly respected South African Jew, would know better than most how difficult it is to achieve real balance in defining this situation. Meanwhile, the President of the United States, in a message to world Jews on the occasion of Rosh Hashanah (the Jewish New Year), has rededicated himself to the security of Israel without ever mentioning Palestine.

All of that is by way of answering a question: Just what do Prime Minister Benyamin Netanyahu and his hard right collaborators have in mind? They are proceeding rapidly on two fronts. No matter what they say, one is to expand both the number of settlements and the Jewish population of the West Bank as rapidly as possible, and subsidize settlers as needed to do this. In the face of US pressure to cease and desist, the goal is rapidly to create new facts on the ground that will be difficult to ignore. The other is to erase or, at the very least, reduce the Arab presence in old Jerusalem. As they have done in many other areas of ancient Palestine, the Israeli scheme is to obliterate the signs of Palestinian history, including some truly historic sites in old Jerusalem, and create on the landscape whatever will serve an ersatz Jewish history.

The underlying tragedy of it all is that ancient communities, both Christian and Muslim, and the physical evidences of their past, and their traditional populations are all being erased in a Zionist effort to create the narrative of a Jewish state. Some families have property ownership documents going back at least as far as the tenth century; thus such erasures are not mere acts of ethnic cleansing—a war crime anywhere else on earth; they are systematic efforts to erase an ancient culture and the evidence of its history—which is a crime against all of human society.

Is the rest of the world truly asleep to this travesty? International media seem locked in providing an Israel-centered and trivial display of these events, one that is only slightly less trivial than the apparent efforts of the Obama team to achieve some visible political success by stopping settlement expansion, even a little bit for a few months. The problem is not really about interrupting the spread of Israelis into Palestinian territory. That would be simple if the Israeli extremists were prepared to accept defined boundaries for Israel and leave the rest of the land to its rightful owners.

Settlements are the most visible manifestation of the Greater Israel dream. They have been its mode of achievement since the first day, and they proceed on the clear appreciation of Israelis on the move that there are no intervening boundaries. Israel simply has not agreed to any permanent boundary around its already illegally acquired part of Palestine, because that would bring the whole show to a defined halt. A temporary halt in building or expanding settlements is simply no substitute for Israeli acceptance that their state is bounded like any other and they must get used to living on the land within those bounds. That alone would be a major legal concession by the Palestinians, because the Israelis stole the land in the first place.

The rest of the world for decades has remained largely silent on this situation. To be sure, the situation is freakish. The lands in question have belonged to Palestinian families for centuries. However, as discussed earlier, in a meeting with George W. Bush in 2004, Israeli Prime Minister Ariel Sharon received a letter from Bush that says—in effect—the Israelis can keep the Palestinian lands they have expanded into illegally. Treatment of that letter in comments of politicians and media stories has suggested that the Bush letter simply unhooked the ownership of lands in Palestine from traditional rules of land title. Nobody, so far, has raised the obvious fact that George W. Bush had no legal right to convey a single square inch of Palestinian land to an Israeli, unless, of course, he was acting, by consent, as the agent of a Palestinian landowner and the owner received appropriate compensation. The tragedy of this situation is that nobody seems prepared to stand up for the rights of the Palestinians. Virtually any place on earth other than Palestine, taking a piece of land in the Israeli manner would be cause for immediate and clear-cut legal rebuttal, if not a gunfight.

It has become easy, it seems, to deal with the Palestinians as non-people. Bush and Sharon didn't consult the Palestinians about transferring their lands to Israelis; they just did it. Netanyahu and his team don't ask the Palestinians in East Jerusalem about whether they want to leave their ancestral homes; they just shove them out. The rest of the world, where land ownership is bounded by rigorous rules, does not object or raise issues of law and fairness. This means basically that the world will tolerate Zionist empire building and will allow deliberate violation of the rights of the Palestinian people to achieve it.

There is an ironic side to this scenario. Virtually all of the Palestinians being mistreated by these processes are Semites. They are the sons of Shem just as the indigenous Jews who are referred to as the "people of the book". The leading Jews who are pressing the case are the Ashkenazim, who are not Semites. There are about ten million people in the ancient Palestine terri-

PALESTINE In Need of a Just God

tory, and they are about equally divided between Israelis and Palestinians. In simple human terms, are the rights of the Jewish side of this population greater and more important than the rights of the Palestinian side of it? Israeli words and actions often say so, but should the rest of the world agree? These are issues that cannot be resolved by tinkering with settlement building, expansion or maintenance. The real questions are: Do the Palestinian people have equal rights in this situation? Do the Palestinians whose ancestors were born and bred on this land have true rights in it? Any answer other than yes would violate basic human rights and the principles of international law. One cannot in good conscience fail to recognize this reality and respond to it without being anti-Semitic.

Meanwhile, how can the situation be rectified? The first rule has to be that in any discussion that seeks to fix the terms of their future, their rights, or the disposition of their property, responsible Palestinian representatives will always be present and will speak for the Palestinian people. The Bush-Sharon type of letter-writing agreement is a travesty of international law and procedure. The second rule is that Bush-Sharon type agreements that did not include the willing participation of Palestinian representatives are scrubbed herewith and cease to be treated as if they have legal standing. The third rule is that any disputes between the Palestinians and the Israelis over property ownership should be mediated by detached third parties, preferably from the UN or the International Court of Justice. The fourth

Terrell E Arnold

rule, of course, is that Israel actually undertakes to control its people, to curb their long established habit of taking what does not belong to them. That means, even at some risk, that invasive settlements of all kinds must stop. The fifth rule is that if Israel refuses to abide by such conditions it should be treated internationally as a rogue state and sanctioned as rigorously as any other state that refuses to behave. None of that would be simple, but it would be about time.

Chapter 28.
Zionists Fabricate as US Digs a Deeper ME Hole

6-5-10

In the days since the Israeli armed forces attacked an unarmed aid convoy in the international waters of the Eastern Mediterranean, Americans have been treated to a growing Israeli fiction: In essence, the Israelis say: "We were merely defending ourselves against invaders. When we invaded their vessels, those people fought back, and we only used force as necessary to defend ourselves." That the attack was unprovoked, and that the vessels attacked were unarmed is glossed over in the same manner that Israeli use of depleted uranium and white phosphorus weapons in the December 2008, January 2009 attacks on Gaza were swept under the rug. With virtually unchallenged access to mainstream media, the Zionists and their supporters are busily wiring together the Israeli version of this assault.

The epitome of apologists is probably Charles Krauthammer in the June 4, 2010 Washington Post piece: "Those Troublesome Jews." A more balanced and historically rooted piece by Uri Avnery, an Israeli activist, puts the Israeli crime squarely on the shoulders of Netanyahu and his Zionist cabinet. Meanwhile Israeli forces have stopped another vessel, the Rachel Corrie and are towing it to shore in a repeat performance.

In failing to react to Monday's attack American leadership has dug itself a hole that now may be deepening. President Obama's excuse is that he was waiting for more information about these tragic events before taking a position. His reaction and those of the great majority of political Washington, especially the Congress, raise real doubts as to whether US leadership appreciates how deadly the Israeli attack was for American interests, and such ignorance seems to have kept it from calling the Israelis to account for this attack.

The accumulating evidence of the US supported 2006 Israeli war against Lebanon, the US supplied Israeli assault on Gaza in December 2008/January 2009, the attack on the Turkish-led aid flotilla, and this morning's reported capture of the Rachel Corrie cast the US in an increasingly unfavorable light. It has become a willing and hardly silent partner in a pattern of regional Israeli military aggression.

These episodes further inflame the festering sores on US policy toward Gaza. In late 2005 the US promoted an election in Palestine in the hope of strengthening the rule of the Fatah Party and the successor to Yasser Arafat. The apparent US reading of the Palestinian situ-

PALESTINE In Need of a Just God

ation was that Arafat's former deputy, Mahmoud Abbas, and his Fatah supporters would be shoo-ins. However, despite the alleged amounts of US and Israeli intelligence operators in the region—backed to be sure by British and other readings—and their financial support for Fatah, the collective outsider view of Palestine was erroneous. The reason was the increasingly important and popular leadership role Hamas had come to play.

Americans, blinded by their view that Hamas was a terrorist organization, have failed to take on board the fact that Hamas, much more solidly than Fatah, understands and represents the interests of the Palestinian people. Moreover, Hamas is both a good political system manager and an honest one. In its posture the US simply bet on the wrong team, and Hamas won the right to rule Palestine. By the estimates of experienced outside observers such as former president Jimmy Carter, the Hamas victory was fair and square.

With a parliamentary majority, Hamas formed a government, but Abbas, with the US and Israel prompting from the sidelines, was not prepared to play. He could be a Palestinian president of Fatah but running the country with a parliamentary majority of Hamas. His decision, apparently shared by the US and Israel, was to split the government, leave Hamas in charge—whatever that would mean—in Gaza, and move the nominal Palestinian seat of government to Ramallah. Ironically, Ramallah had been, by Israeli design and enforcement, Yasser Arafat's pre-demise prison in the

West Bank. While he is free to come and go on Israeli/US approved errands, Abbas has become a very similar prisoner.

The scenario for this gambit was to make Abbas and his Fatah following comfortable in the West Bank, protect them well from possible political enfilading by Hamas that has considerable following in the West Bank as well, and basically ignore the Palestinians under Hamas in Gaza. Abbas obviously was afraid that he lacked the political following to defeat Hamas in an electoral gambit. Thus, the solution was to enjoy the comforts of a protected, basically Israeli/American controlled environment in the West Bank, and let Hamas cope as well as it might with the stringencies of life in an isolated Gaza.

Hamas proved impossible to dislodge in Gaza. While Israel and its US masters in the West Bank made Abbas and his followers comfortable, the pressure on Hamas and Gaza was unrelenting. Meanwhile, if much less than perfectly, Hamas was coping for the people in Gaza. Their principal tool was smuggling which, as any Middle East hand knows, is the most common way of doing business in many border areas. Despite an onerous Israeli blockade, the Gaza Palestinians, aided and abetted by established trans-border tunnels and smugglers in the Mediterranean and in the border regions of Egypt, managed to survive.

PALESTINE In Need of a Just God

Gaza became a complex political agenda. Abbas knew he and his Fatah party could not defeat Hamas candidates in a fair election, and a Fatah attempt militarily to unseat Hamas failed. Israeli leaders knew that Hamas articulated the central Palestinian agenda far more clearly than Fatah. That meant Hamas stood for the primary Palestinian agenda including (a) the right of return for Palestinians, (b) compensation for Palestinians whose lands in Israel had been confiscated by Israelis, (c) a two state solution with at least all the territory in the Gaza and West Bank territories represented by the 1967 truce line, and (d) a Palestinian capital in East Jerusalem. In that context, Hamas would recognize Israel when Israel recognized Palestine.

All of that was pure anathema to the proponents of Greater Israel. Scaled down to the possible dimensions of the 21st century, Greater Israel would be the territory between the Mediterranean and the Jordan River. There was no room in it for Palestinians. The fact that the proponents of Greater Israel, really the Ashkenazim Khazars of Central Europe, were neither ethnic Jews nor people of the book did not interfere with their aim to claim the whole of Palestine. That dream map included some pieces that belong to Lebanon, Syria, Jordan, and Egypt.

Meanwhile, Egyptian leadership would be happy to dispose of Hamas, since it sprang from a political faction in Egypt (the Muslim Brotherhood) that has become increasingly popular. Given half a chance this group, the Brotherhood, along with other oppositionists, would grow into a full-fledged political challenge to the ruling elite. The Egyptian republic, which is essentially a closed dynastic system, was founded in 1953 by Mohamed Naguib. He was followed shortly by Gamal Abdel Nasser and Egypt has been blessed by only two captains since—Anwar el Sadat who was assassinated in 1981, and Hosni Mubarak who, after almost thirty years in power, is presently trying to pass the mantle to his son. The possibility of an elected Hamas-like government elected by the people of Egypt does not sit well with the Mubarak oligarchs. Thus Hamas, as a political force in Gaza is an attractive nuisance to the present Egyptian regime.

In this complex of Palestinian political separatism, Israeli ambition to gain the whole of Palestine, Egyptian desires to limit, if not eradicate, the political force represented by Hamas, and the desires of surrounding countries eventually to lose their Palestinian refugee populations, the unpleasant events of the past few years have transpired. The political success of Hamas was a severe shock to many in the neighborhood, but Hamas has proved politically more acceptable to Arab governments than Fatah. In addition, the United States, having billed Hamas as a terrorist group because it attacks Israel, especially in the border areas of Gaza, seems determined not to recognize Hamas as a viable political force, no matter how well it takes care of its charges in Gaza.

PALESTINE In Need of a Just God

The Israeli attacks on the Turkish led deliverers of assistance to Gaza are inevitably entangled in that history. Muted or non-existent reactions to Israeli excesses in dealing with Gaza suggest that the Zionists can proceed with their Greater Israel campaign without serious outside interference. By preventing the people of Gaza from rebuilding, while trying to starve them into leaving, Gaza can be retained as part of Greater Israel. Moreover, any Palestinian resistance to this process will be dismissed as terrorism or simply ignored.

The United States has been unable to take a detached stance on the flotilla attacks because its leadership is too deeply in bed with the Israelis as well as ideologically indisposed to consider Hamas a viable Palestinian political force. Even polite Israeli society would be more comfortable if there were no Palestinians in Gaza. Israeli leadership fears Hamas because it defines a Palestinian agenda that would be the death of any concept of Greater Israel. Mahmoud Abbas, at least moderately comfortable under Israeli and US protection in the West Bank, would not mourn the end of Hamas rule in Gaza even if it were to result from stopping the flotillas of assistance that help keep the people of Gaza alive.

The Israeli goal is to keep the Palestinian society in Gaza from getting back on its feet. Apologists say that all the aid-giving groups have to do is land the stuff in Israel and the Israelis will deliver it to Gaza. But Israel now permits only about a quarter of the necessary supplies of food and medicine—but no building materials—to enter Gaza. Rebuilding would give the Palestinians a permanence that simply is inconsistent with making room for Greater Israel. In that context, we can expect continuing Israel Defense Force efforts to limit or prevent assistance to Gaza.

Meanwhile the Palestinian people, ever more tightly crowded into shrinking Bantustans of land in the West Bank, see their chances for a Palestinian homeland daily diminished by Israeli land confiscation. The Israeli settlements of recent mention can happen only by confiscating more land from its Palestinian owners. Wealthy Americans who are credited by Israelis with generously spending their money to expand settlements have to know that the land belongs to Palestinians who are not paid for it. In this context, many well-meaning people—Turkish , American, Muslim country, European, and others—find their efforts to help the Palestinian people frustrated by attackers whose agenda includes the eventual elimination of all Palestinians from the Holy Land. The Israeli attacks on the aid flotillas are only the recent crimes in this long brewing tragedy.

Chapter 29.
The Road to Middle East Peace

Ever since the Palestinian elections of January 2006, the search for peace in the Middle East has been like the legendary chimpanzee's typewriter creation of Shakespeare—a random pecking at the political keyboard that never finishes a sentence. In 2006 Israel thought it might improve the climate for peace on its own terms, so it invaded Lebanon to eliminate Hezbollah, one of the major sources of support for Hamas and the Palestinian people. The Israel Defense Force (IDF) devastated Lebanon, but the assault only strengthened Hezbollah into a leading light of the present Lebanese government. Since "Hezbollah" means Party of God, the party entered fully and successfully into Lebanese politics.

Under cover of its invasion of Lebanon, the IDF also increased hectoring of the Palestinians in Gaza. Refusing to accept the elections that gave Hamas the right to form a new Palestinian government, Israel and the US then set out to keep Mahmoud Abbas and his Fatah party in power. Hamas preferred formation of a unity government, but, under pressure from the US and the Israelis, Abbas and his Fatah party wanted no part of it. Having failed to overturn Hamas in a pitched battle, Fatah found that the power it had lost in a free election could not be regained militarily. The US-Israeli solution was to move Abbas and the Fatah leadership to Ramallah in the West Bank in 2007 and to help Abbas create a government without Hamas, without an election, and therefore, if challenged, without legitimacy.

Abbas established a government in Ramallah with a US/Israeli mandate. He did not have the nerve to ask the Palestinian people for one, because, had he done so, Hamas (if it were allowed to enter candidates) probably retained enough support in the West Bank to again win the lead. The situation was hardly made to order for a "free" election, so Abbas didn't hold one. In the meantime, Abbas erected his government in Ramallah within the enfolding arms of Israeli perimeter protection/confinement, Mossad coverage of possible flies in the ointment (including any Hamas effort to assert its majority political power in the West Bank), and US training/control of security forces for the Abbas government. Gaza and the pesky Hamas crowd could simply be ignored.

That might have worked as the order of the day, except that there were 1.5 million people (more than one of every three Palestinians in Palestine) in Gaza under Hamas rule. Tightening the cordon around Gaza was the first Israeli effort to eliminate Hamas. Abbas and

PALESTINE In Need of a Just God

Fatah fully approved. Maybe, thought the Israelis, if life became hard enough for the people in Gaza they would abandon Hamas. To that end, Israel instituted tight control of Gaza borders, ran intensive patrols of coastal waters and had Egyptian dictator Hosni Mobarak's support for rigorous control of Palestinian movements through the city of Rafah gateway into Egypt. However, these strictures appear to have yielded better, even motor vehicle sized Palestinian tunnels into Egypt from Gaza and probably more stubborn swimmers, because Gaza did not collapse. The Gaza Palestinians and their Hamas leadership proved very stubborn.

Then, in a second effort, in December 2008 the IDF launched what it called Operation Cast Lead to disassemble Gaza and pull the rug from under Hamas. The IDF is one of the best armed military forces in the world (thanks in great measure to outright gifts of American money and equipment). It lined up against Palestinian militias equipped with small arms and rockets—most of them crude and handmade.

Bombing and strafing without concern for civilian casualties, by the end of January 2009 the IDF had made a shambles of what was left (after years of restrictions) of Gaza's infrastructure. The IDF killed about 1500 Palestinians and wounded about 4500—mostly women and children.

The people of Gaza emerged from Operation Cast Lead battered but unbowed. In fact, recently the United

Terrell E Arnold

Nations Relief and Works Agency (UNRWA) reported that the five year Israeli blockade had made life miserable for the Palestinians, but it had empowered Hamas. (See: UNRWA "Labor Market Briefing, Gaza Strip", June 2011).

Over following weeks and months private and multinational efforts to provide assistance to Gaza increased, especially efforts to supply Gaza by sea. Israeli attacks to stop those supplies led to the June 7, 2010 IDF assault—in international waters—on the unarmed Turkish vessel, Mavi Marmara, and others that caused at least 9 deaths of Mavi Marmara crewmen and other injured. However, those attacks did not stop the efforts to supply Gaza by sea.

To Israel's frustration, despite their on the ground situation, the Palestinians in Gaza were simply not prepared to call it quits. Meanwhile, Abbas and his Fatah followers huddled in the relatively comfortable environs of polite US/Israeli captivity.

It was in this nearly totally dysfunctional political environment that the US decided it was time (again) for the Israelis and the Palestinians to hold "direct" peace talks. Indirect talks had occurred from time to time for years in the total absence of any agenda or any real results. It was decided to proceed anyway without the participation or representation of a third of the Palestinian people: Hamas, whose candidates had won control of the Palestine People's Assembly, and those poor beleaguered souls in Gaza would neither be consulted nor invited. It must be emphasized that the only way either the Palestinians or the Israelis could be brought to the table was without any commitments in advance. Without anything on the table on either side, talks were to have begun in September 2010.

To be fair, Abbas did not appear unmindful of the limitations posed by the absence of Hamas. He remained legally in power until late 2010, and he was not challenged when he remained in power after the end of his term, but the Fatah government he had formed represented only a minority, while the last legally elected government of Palestine remained in Gaza and, as noted above, it was not invited to those talks.

With an honest broker on the scene, Mahmoud Abbas could possibly have been the representative of all the Palestinians in any new talks. However, he was too avidly supporting US/Israeli efforts to eliminate Hamas to have any integrity. With the Barak Obama White House unequivocally on the side of the Israelis, and with the US Congress blatantly under the control of AIPAC (The American Israel Public Affairs Committee), the Palestinians had little to no chance of being heard.

Actual Israeli and Palestinian positions were thoroughly dug in. The Israelis made their position crystal clear. Before arriving in Washington for a May 19, 2009 meeting with President Obama, Prime Minister Netanyahu said that Israel would not commit to any concessions on territory. While he did not put it that way, the increasingly clear official Israeli goal was to acquire all of Palestine without any Palestinians. Therefore, virtually no one in Israeli leadership wanted to talk about an actual peace agreement.

On the other side, Abbas would have lost any remaining credibility he had with Palestinians if he did not echo the Hamas position. At minimum, Hamas subscribed to the Arab League formula. That formula, floated in Beirut in 2002 and credited to Saudi Arabian Crown Prince (now King) Abdullah, is worth repeating in this final chapter. The Beirut formula would require Israel to back off to the 1967 truce line, agree to return or compensation for expelled Palestinians, agree to a Palestinian capital in East Jerusalem, help create a truly independent Palestinian state, and recognize the rights of the Palestinian people. In exchange, Palestine would recognize Israel's right to exist with borders along the 1967 truce line. As optimists might have said, things could have improved with discussion, but on the issues as stated, the chances were close to zero that any real discussion would occur.

Most world governments hoped, it appears, that the United States actually would mediate this situation. However, the crude reality was that the United States was not positioned to carry out a mediator role. President Obama had to know the Israeli refusal to make any present concessions had stalled Middle East peace talks for more than a generation. Obama also had to know that this was the only foreign policy issue that could cause him to lose the next election. This, he knew, had become a so-called "third rail" of American politics. Trying to force the Israelis to make any real concessions would be a politically costly maneuver. Moreover, he was well aware of the strenuous constraints on his freedom of action that would be imposed by an almost perfectly pro-Israeli Congress. The question was whether he was determined enough to get some results as well as bold enough to take the kinds of political chances that any substantial outcome from these talks would require.

Netanyahu and Obama had agreed on talks to start in June 2010 (Note, the Palestinians were apparently not in on that agreement). However, Israel became concerned about the international backlash from the IDF assault on the Mavi Marmara, and Netanyahu deferred the talks. Obama attempted in late 2010 to restart them, but the Israelis, especially Netanyahu, could not be reeled in.

Obama and Netanyahu finally met again on the subject in May 2011, but by that time, two critical events had occurred. First, the Palestinians had decided to take the issue of statehood to the UN in September. That decision was flatly rejected by Netanyahu who said such a move would "delegitimize" Israel. That charge was totally without logic, but Obama agreed. That Israel had delegitimized itself long ago through abuse of the Palestinians and land theft to create and grow Israel, most recently in the Israeli-occupied West Bank, was simply ignored.

Second, in a May 4 Cairo meeting brokered by the Egyptians, Mahmoud Abbas, representing Fatah, and Khaled Mesha'al, the political leader of Hamas, reached an agreement to form a new Palestinian unity government. This was seen by the Palestinians and most observers in the outside world as an essential and positive step toward peace. However, Netanyahu and his government wanted no part of a Fatah-Hamas unity government, and Obama—characteristically—sided with him. So far as these two were concerned, Hamas remained a terrorist group, and its political success as well as its effective and sustained management of a truce with the Israelis counted for naught.

Under the Abbas-Mesha'al agreement, a caretaker government of technocrats would prepare for national elections in 2012. In the run-up period, however it might be worked out with the Israelis, candidates would be chosen in both the West Bank and Gaza. Undoubtedly, any new peace talks would have to be deferred until that new government came into power. How the deal would bear on Palestinian relations with Israel or the prospect of resuming peace talks was unclear. But in any case, putting the statehood issue to the UN was viewed by both Obama and Netanyahu as politically offensive. Thus peace talks, which in any case Netanyahu clearly did not want, were deferred to the indefinite future.

PALESTINE In Need of a Just God

Such was Obama's Babylonian captivity. He was the President of the most powerful military power on the planet. However, unless he was prepared to take extreme domestic political risks, he lacked the political power to control management of this issue even in his own capital. Washington, where Israel-Palestine issues were concerned, was under the political control of Zionists and their American Christian, Neocon and Jewish supporters. Every President from Harry Truman onward had confronted some version of this political dilemma, but none could have seen it presented more forcefully.

Today US prestige in the Middle East is at low ebb, while the scope of legitimate American interests—notably vis-a-vis energy—is at least a demanding long term constant. For decades the United States has been tagged with the task of achieving a settlement between Israel and the Palestinians. For decades the Israelis have worked openly and steadily to steal Palestine from its owners. They have remained free to do so in part because they have used their domestic US sources of support to keep US leadership in a political straitjacket where Israeli interests are concerned. That the process has been progressive grand theft of homes, properties and lives has been virtually ignored by the outside world. Israeli access to and control of media has enabled them to put the blame on Palestine, but that fog is slowly clearing as more people become aware of the facts of Israeli land theft and ethnic cleansing of Palestine. US credibility hangs by a thread of hope that it will become an honest broker and, for once, treat the Palestinians as equals of the Israelis.

This is the part of the situation that is different for President Barak Obama. The world has become more aware of Middle East reality, and Americans increasingly confront it. The American people are increasingly mindful of the human cruelty and injustice built into Israel's aggressive creation of a Jewish state by land theft and confiscation. Under a regime of military occupation, Palestine is being picked apart by IDF designs on the Jordan River border with Jordan and by Israeli settlers who simply take the land they want and shove out Palestinian owners. Through Internet, small stream and independent media, more Americans are becoming aware of our country's Israel support role in this ongoing crime against humanity.

American leadership can be faulted for its failures to lead on resolution of this conflict. However, the design of a peace agreement between an invader and its victims is not your run of the mill diplomatic venture, especially when the politically powerful invader persists in blaming the situation on the victims. After six decades of land confiscation and collective punishment of the Palestinian victims, getting the Palestinians to take seriously the idea of peace talks is itself no simple matter.

Herein lies Obama's problem. All of the players are not present. Not even the last fairly elected majority party is on the scene. To attempt a binding agreement when the President of Palestine is himself now unelected, when one of the parties is not represented legally, and in this case, the last freely elected Palestinian government is forcefully excluded, is at least novel diplomatic terrain. On the other hand, the peace process that goes nowhere is tailor made for Israeli Zionist leadership that seeks to avoid any concessions or agreement. No peace agreement simply means more time for the Israelis to steal more of Palestine.

President Obama's chosen Middle East peace negotiator, former Senator George Mitchell, searched unsuccessfully for two years for a real mandate to broker Middle East peace talks. Having failed to define or to acquire such a mandate, he resigned on May 13, 2011. Unfortunately, with his resignation the American public lost a negotiator who knew whereof he spoke. When accepting the Liberty Medal in 1998, for his work on the Belfast accord, United States Special Envoy for Northern Ireland, Mitchell said "I believe there's no such thing as a conflict that can't be ended…No matter how ancient the conflict, no matter how hateful, no matter how hurtful, peace can prevail. But only if those who stand for peace and justice are supported and encouraged, while those who do not are opposed and condemned. Seeking an end to conflict is not for the timid or the tentative…" The Middle East situation offers perhaps the ultimate test of his reasoning.

Terrell E Arnold

The awkward truth is that as this book goes to press the future of Middle East peace is being prejudiced by a persistent double standard. When the Zionists wanted to create the state of Israel, they set about taking the lands away from the Palestinian people. They then declared Israel a state—without asking anybody whether they could do it. To gain acceptance, and over the objections of several senior Federal officials, they made a politically life threatening attack on President Harry Truman at the White House to get the US to be the first country to recognize the new state. The UN acquiesced. Thus Israel came into being.

Now the Palestinians are scheduled to ask the United Nations to admit Palestine as a member state. This is as correct a path for the Palestinians as it was in 1948 for the Israelis. They plan to do this at the September 2011 meetings of the UN General Assembly. The Israelis are pressing the United States and others who will listen to block this effort; their perverse argument is that admitting Palestine to the UN would "delegitimize" Israel. The Saudis have come out strongly in favor of a US move to accept Palestinian statehood.

Declaration of a Palestinian state is not per se contrary to real Israeli interests. It is in fact entirely consistent with the UN partition decision that made room in Palestine for the new state of Israel. However, hardline Israeli leadership wants it blocked because declaring a State of Palestine would end forever the Zionist dream

PALESTINE In Need of a Just God

of a Greater Israel that would become an exclusively Jewish state.

Many Palestinians and many Israelis see a declaration of Palestinian statehood to be the binding premise on which peace may finally come to the Palestinian people and to the people of Israel. Statehood now has the enthusiastic support of the great majority of the world's people. Hopefully, the compassionate people Americans are, aided by a just God, will help bring that about.

ANNEXES

I.
The Balfour Declaration of Great Britain

Foreign Office,
November 2nd, 1917.

Dear Lord Rothschild,
I have much pleasure in conveying to you, on behalf of His Majesty's Government, the following declaration of sympathy with Jewish Zionist aspirations which has been submitted to, and approved by, the Cabinet:

"His Majesty's Government view with favour the establishment in Palestine of a national home for the Jewish people, and will use their best endeavours to facilitate the achievement of this object, it being clearly understood that nothing shall be done which may prejudice the civil and religious rights of existing non-Jewish communities in Palestine, or the rights and political status enjoyed by Jews in any other country".

I should be grateful if you would bring this declaration to the knowledge of the Zionist Federation.

Yours sincerely
Arthur James Balfour

II.
President George W. Bush letter to Israeli Prime Minister Ariel Sharon

April 14, 2004

Dear Mr. Prime Minister:

Thank you for your letter setting out your disengagement plan.

The United States remains hopeful and determined to find a way forward toward a resolution of the Israeli-Palestinian dispute. I remain committed to my June 24, 2002 vision of two states living side by side in peace and security as the key to peace, and to the roadmap as the route to get there.

We welcome the disengagement plan you have prepared, under which Israel would withdraw certain military installations and all settlements from Gaza, and withdraw certain military installations and settlements in the West Bank. These steps described in the plan will mark real progress toward realizing my June 24, 2002 vision, and make a real contribution towards peace. We also understand that, in this context, Israel believes it is important to bring new opportunities to the

Negev and the Galilee. We are hopeful that steps pursuant to this plan, consistent with my vision, will remind all states and parties of their own obligations under the roadmap.

The United States appreciates the risks such an undertaking represents. I therefore want to reassure you on several points. First, the United States remains committed to my vision and to its implementation as described in the roadmap. The United States will do its utmost to prevent any attempt by anyone to impose any other plan. Under the roadmap, Palestinians must undertake an immediate cessation of armed activity and all acts of violence against Israelis anywhere, and all official Palestinian institutions must end incitement against Israel. The Palestinian leadership must act decisively against terror, including sustained, targeted, and effective operations to stop terrorism and dismantle terrorist capabilities and infrastructure. Palestinians must undertake a comprehensive and fundamental political reform that includes a strong parliamentary democracy and an empowered prime minister.

Second, there will be no security for Israelis or Palestinians until they and all states, in the region and beyond, join together to fight terrorism and dismantle terrorist organizations.... The United States reiterates its steadfast commitment to Israel's security, including secure, defensible borders, and to preserve and strengthen Israel's capability to deter and defend itself, by itself, against any threat or possible combination of threats.

Third, Israel will retain its right to defend itself against terrorism, including to take actions against terrorist organizations.... The United States understands that after Israel withdraws from Gaza and/or parts of the West Bank, and pending agreements on other arrangements, existing arrangements regarding control of airspace, territorial waters, and land pas-

PALESTINE In Need of a Just God

sages of the West Bank and Gaza will continue. The United States is strongly committed to Israel's security and well-being as a Jewish state. It seems clear that an agreed, just, fair, and realistic framework for a solution to the Palestinian refugee issue as part of any final status agreement will need to be found through the establishment of a Palestinian state, and the settling of Palestinian refugees there, rather than in Israel.

As part of a final peace settlement, Israel must have secure and recognized borders, which should emerge from negotiations between the parties in accordance with UNSC Resolutions 242 and 338. In light of new realities on the ground, including already existing major Israeli populations centers, it is unrealistic to expect that the outcome of final status negotiations will be a full and complete return to the armistice lines of 1949, and all previous efforts to negotiate a two-state solution have reached the same conclusion. It is realistic to expect that any final status agreement will only be achieved on the basis of mutually agreed changes that reflect these realities.

I know that, as you state in your letter, you are aware that certain responsibilities face the State of Israel. Among these, your government has stated that the barrier being erected by Israel should be a security rather than political barrier, should be temporary rather than permanent, and therefore not prejudice any final status issues including final borders, and its route should take into account, consistent with security needs, its impact on Palestinians not engaged in terrorist activities. As you know, the United States supports the establishment of a Palestinian state that is viable, contiguous, sovereign, and independent, so that the Palestinian people can build their own future in accordance with my vision set forth in June 2002 and with the path set forth in the roadmap....

Terrell E Arnold

A peace settlement negotiated between Israelis and Palestinians would be a great boon not only to those peoples but to the peoples of the entire region. Accordingly, the United States believes that all states in the region have special responsibilities: to support the building of the institutions of a Palestinian state; to fight terrorism, and cut off all forms of assistance to individuals and groups engaged in terrorism; and to begin now to move toward more normal relations with the State of Israel. These actions would be true contributions to building peace in the region.

Mr. Prime Minister, you have described a bold and historic initiative that can make an important contribution to peace. I commend your efforts and your courageous decision which I support. As a close friend and ally, the United States intends to work closely with you to help make it a success.

Sincerely,
George W. Bush

III.
Israeli Prime Minister Ariel Sharon letter to President George W. Bush

April 14, 2004

Dear Mr. President,

The vision that you articulated in your 24 June 2002 address constitutes one of the most significant contributions toward ensuring a bright future for the Middle East. Accordingly, the State of Israel has accepted the Roadmap, as adopted by our government. For the first time, a practical and just formula was presented for the achievement of peace, opening a genuine window of opportunity for progress toward a settlement between Israel and the Palestinians, involving two states living side-by-side in peace and security.

This formula sets forth the correct sequence and principles for the attainment of peace. Its full implementation represents the sole means to make genuine progress. As you have stated, a Palestinian state will never be created by terror, and Palestinians must engage in a sustained fight against the terrorists and dismantle their infrastructure. Moreover, there must be serious

Terrell E Arnold

efforts to institute true reform and real democracy and liberty, including new leaders not compromised by terror. We are committed to this formula as the only avenue through which an agreement can be reached. We believe that this formula is the only viable one.

The Palestinian Authority under its current leadership has taken no action to meet its responsibilities under the Roadmap. Terror has not ceased, reform of the Palestinian security services has not been undertaken, and real institutional reforms have not taken place. The State of Israel continues to pay the heavy cost of constant terror. Israel must preserve its capability to protect itself and deter its enemies, and we thus retain our right to defend ourselves against terrorism and to take actions against terrorist organizations.

Having reached the conclusion that, for the time being, there exists no Palestinian partner with whom to advance peacefully toward a settlement and since the current impasse is unhelpful to the achievement of our shared goals, I have decided to initiate a process of gradual disengagement with the hope of reducing friction between Israelis and Palestinians. The Disengagement Plan is designed to improve security for Israel and stabilize our political and economic situation. It will enable us to deploy our forces more effectively until such time that conditions in the Palestinian Authority allow for the full implementation of the Roadmap to resume.

I attach, for your review, the main principles of the Disengagement Plan. This initiative, which we are not undertaking under the roadmap, represents an independent Israeli plan, yet is not inconsistent with the roadmap. According to this plan, the State of Israel intends to relocate military installations and all Israeli villages and towns in the Gaza Strip, as well as other

PALESTINE In Need of a Just God

military installations and a small number of villages in Samaria.

In this context, we also plan to accelerate construction of the Security Fence, whose completion is essential in order to ensure the security of the citizens of Israel. The fence is a security rather than political barrier, temporary rather than permanent, and therefore will not prejudice any final status issues including final borders. The route of the Fence, as approved by our Government's decisions, will take into account, consistent with security needs, its impact on Palestinians not engaged in terrorist activities.

Upon my return from Washington, I expect to submit this Plan for the approval of the Cabinet and the Knesset, and I firmly believe that it will win such approval.

The Disengagement Plan will create a new and better reality for the State of Israel, enhance its security and economy, and strengthen the fortitude of its people. In this context, I believe it is important to bring new opportunities to the Negev and the Galilee. Additionally, the Plan will entail a series of measures with the inherent potential to improve the lot of the Palestinian Authority, providing that it demonstrates the wisdom to take advantage of this opportunity. The execution of the Disengagement Plan holds the prospect of stimulating positive changes within the Palestinian Authority that might create the necessary conditions for the resumption of direct negotiations.

We view the achievement of a settlement between Israel and the Palestinians as our central focus and are committed to realizing this objective. Progress toward this goal must be anchored exclusively in the Roadmap and we will oppose any other plan.

Terrell E Arnold

In this regard, we are fully aware of the responsibilities facing the State of Israel. These include limitations on the growth of settlements; removal of unauthorized outposts; and steps to increase, to the extent permitted by security needs, freedom of movement for Palestinians not engaged in terrorism. Under separate cover we are sending to you a full description of the steps the State of Israel is taking to meet all its responsibilities.

The government of Israel supports the United States efforts to reform the Palestinian security services to meet their roadmap obligations to fight terror. Israel also supports the American's efforts, working with the International Community, to promote the reform process, build institutions and improve the economy of the Palestinian Authority and to enhance the welfare of its people, in the hope that a new Palestinian leadership will prove able to fulfill its obligations under the roadmap.

I want to again express my appreciation for your courageous leadership in the war against global terror, your important initiative to revitalize the Middle East as a more fitting home for its people and, primarily, your personal friendship and profound support for the State of Israel.

Sincerely,
Ariel Sharon

IV.
Gist of Concurrent House/Senate Resolution

House, Senate Back Sharon Disengagement Plan
(June 23-24, 2004)

The Senate voted June 24, 2004, to embrace President Bush's support of Israeli Prime Minister Ariel Sharon's plan to withdraw from the Gaza Strip. The Senate's action came a day after the House approved a similar measure by a 407-9 roll call vote.

The concurrent resolution states that Congress: (1) strongly endorses the principles articulated by President Bush in his letter dated April 14, 2004, to Israeli Prime Minister Ariel Sharon which will strengthen the security and well-being of the State of Israel; and (2) supports continuing efforts with the international community to build the capacity and will of Palestinian institutions to fight terrorism, dismantle terrorist organizations, and prevent the areas from which Israel has withdrawn from posing a threat to the security of Israel.

By 95-3, Senators approved nonbinding language that also said "it is unrealistic" for any peace settlement between Israel and Palestinians to require Israel to return to the borders that existed before the 1967 war. In addition, the resolution

Terrell E Arnold

said a Palestinian state would have to be part of a "just, fair and realistic framework" for peace with Palestinian refugees settling there, not in Israel. The Senate resolution said Palestinians must stop "armed activity and all acts of violence against Israelis anywhere."

Both chambers' resolutions endorsed Bush's April 14 letter to Sharon in which Bush backed Sharon's plan to remove Jewish settlements and some military installations from Gaza, and some military bases and settlements from the West Bank.

V
United Nations Security Council Resolution 242

22 November 1967

The Security Council,

Expressing its continuing concern with the grave situation in the Middle East,

Emphasizing the inadmissibility of the acquisition of territory by war and the need to work for a just and lasting peace in which every State in the area can live in security,

Emphasizing further that all Member States in their acceptance of the Charter of the United Nations have undertaken a commitment to act in accordance with Article 2 of the Charter,

1. *Affirms* that the fulfilment of Charter principles requires the establishment of a just and lasting peace in the Middle East which should include the application of both the following principles:

Terrell E Arnold

(i) Withdrawal of Israel armed forces from territories occupied in the recent conflict;

(ii) Termination of all claims or states of belligerency and respect for and acknowledgment of the sovereignty, territorial integrity and political independence of every State in the area and their right to live in peace within secure and recognized boundaries free from threats or acts of force;

2. *Affirms further* the necessity

(a) For guaranteeing freedom of navigation through international waterways in the area;

(b) For achieving a just settlement of the refugee problem;

(c) For guaranteeing the territorial inviolability and political independence of every State in the area, through measures including the establishment of demilitarized zones;

3. *Requests* the Secretary-General to designate a Special Representative to proceed to the Middle East to establish and maintain contacts with the States concerned in order to promote agreement and assist efforts to achieve a peaceful and accepted settlement in accordance with the provisions and principles in this resolution;

4. *Requests* the Secretary-General to report to the Security Council on the progress of the efforts of the Special Representative as soon as possible.

Adopted unanimously at the 1382nd meeting.

VI
United Nations Security Council Resolution 338

22 October 1973

The Security Council

1. Calls upon all parties to the present fighting to cease all firing and terminate all military activity immediately, no later than 12 hours after the moment of the adoption of this decision, in the positions they now occupy;

2. Calls upon the parties concerned to start immediately after the cease-fire the implementation of Security Council resolution 242 (1967) in all of its parts;

3. Decides that, immediately and concurrently with the cease-fire, negotiations shall start between the parties concerned under appropriate auspices aimed at establishing a just and durable peace in the Middle East.

Adopted at the 1747th meeting by 14 votes to none. 1/

_____

1/ one member (China) did not participate in the voting.

VII.
Congressman Ron Paul's Statement of July 6, 2011

Regarding the Congressional resolution (HR 268) opposing the Palestinian statehood initiative in the U.N. and opposing Hamas-Fatah reconciliation: <u>Reaffirming the United States commitment to a negotiated settlement of the Israeli-Palestinian conflict through direct Israeli-Palestinian negotiations, and for other purposes.</u>

Mr. Speaker I rise in opposition to this resolution. While I certainly share the hope for peace in the Middle East and a solution to the ongoing conflict, I do not believe that peace will result if we continue to do the same things while hoping for different results. The US has been involved in this process for decades, spending billions of dollars we do not have, yet we never seem to get much closer to a solution. I believe the best solution is to embrace non-interventionism, which allows those most directly involved to solve their own problems.

This resolution not only further entangles the US in the Israeli/Palestinian dispute, but it sets out the kind of outcome the United States would accept in advance. While I prefer our disengagement from that conflict, I

Terrell E Arnold

must wonder how the US expects to be seen as an "honest broker" when it dictates the terms of a solution in such a transparently one-sided manner.

In the resolution before us, all demands are made of only one side in the conflict. Do supporters of this resolution really believe the actors in the Middle East and the rest of the world do not notice? We do no favors to the Israelis or to the Palestinians when we involve ourselves in such a manner and block any negotiations that may take place without US participation. They have the incentives to find a way to live in peace and we must allow them to find that solution on their own. As always, congressional attitudes toward the peace process in the Middle East reveal hubris and self-importance. Only those who must live together in the Middle East can craft a lasting peace between Israel and Palestine.

VIII
Biographic Sketches:

Mahmoud Abbas: Known often by his war name of Abu Mazen. In the 1960s he worked with Yasser Arafat in creating the Palestine Liberation Organization and its terrorist arm, Fatah. He was elected to succeed Arafat as President of the Palestinian Authority when the founder died in 2005, and he is presently the leader of Fatah, which—long retired from terrorism—has become Palestine's largest political party. He is now serving as President, although his term has expired, and reportedly he has indicated he would not seek reelection.

Marwan Barghouti: One of leading and most popular Palestinian Fatah Party loyalists. He was arrested by the Israelis in 2003, tried and sentenced in 2004 to five consecutive life sentences for alleged killing of Israeli civilians. The son of a West Bank farmer, Barghouti joined Fatah at age 15. He worked for Arafat on the 1993 Oslo Accords. He is often cited as a probable successor to Mahmoud Abbas as leader of the Palestinian Authority, although it is doubtful the Israelis would release him if elected.

Khaled Mesha'al: Operating from Damascus, Syria, Mesha'al has served as the Political Director of Hamas for more than fifteen years. In a recent series of articles in the Jordanian newspaper Al Sabeel, Mesha'al emerges as a clear-headed political thinker, a realist about Palestine's situation and someone who can recruit support for the Hamas cause which appears to have strengthened since the Israelis tried to stifle it by invasions of the Gaza Strip in mid-2006, again in 2008-09, and more recently in aggressive skirmishes.

Salaam Fayad: Presently acting Prime Minister of the Palestinian Authority, ruling from Ramallah in the West Bank. He was appointed to this position in 2009 after Mahmoud Abbas and his Fatah party rejected the parliamentary election victory of Hamas, and—with US and Israeli help—moved the center of the Palestinian Authority to Ramallah and left Hamas out of the de facto government.

Ismail Haniyeh: Named Prime Minister of Palestine in the government formed by Hamas after its victories in the Palestinian Peoples' Assembly elections of January 2006. His appointment was arbitrarily terminated by Mahmoud Abbas who appointed Fayad to the post. When Abbas moved the government to Ramallah, with US and Israeli blessings, he simply terminated the Hamas role in government except in the Gaza Strip.

Ileana Ros-Lehtinen: Cuban-American born member of the US House of Representatives from Florida. A Republican, she is the most senior woman in the House, and she chairs the influential House Foreign Affairs Committee. Together with Congressman Tom Lantos of California, she sponsored the Palestinian Democracy Support Act, a congressional resolution against Hamas leadership of the government.

Thomas Peter (Tom) Lantos: Member of the House of Representatives from California. Now deceased, Lantos was the only Holocaust survivor to serve in the US Congress. As a Member of Congress from 1981 to his death in 2008, he was a strong supporter for the state of Israel and for human rights globally.

Made in the USA
Charleston, SC
28 February 2012